FEELINGS!

FEELINGS!

Where They
Come From
and
How to
Handle Them

JOAN JACOBS

TYNDALE
House Publishers, Inc.
Wheaton, Illinois

COVERDALE
House Publishers Ltd.
Eastbourne, England

Scripture quotations are from the Revised Standard Version of the Bible,
unless otherwise identified.

Library of Congress Catalog Card Number 76-275-73.
ISBN 0-8423-0856-3, paper.
Copyright © 1976 Tyndale House Publishers,
Wheaton Illinois. All rights reserved.
Second printing, December 1976.
Printed in the United States of America.

To Marvin
husband, lover, friend

Contents

I have enjoyed writing about feelings because it has been an experience of personal growth. Almost everything I know about feelings is in these pages. I say *almost*, because I keep learning. Confidence in committing all this to paper came out of the discovery that my needs and experiences reflect those of many others around me.

Preface

Those who accompany me through these chapters will discover that accepting new insights is a slow, filtering process. Using new skills in handling feelings requires persistence. Changing our patterns of being human takes time.

This book is about only one aspect of Christian behavior, attitudes, and relationships. Although I think that what I've said is true to Scripture, whatever is doctrinal is here only to support the book's theme. It is a call to Christians to become aware of their feelings and to use them toward growing in faith.

I like writing acknowledgments because the people who helped are each important to me personally. Dr. Clifford Penner and Dr. Joseph Venema encouraged me from the beginning with their insights. They are clinical psychologists in private practice with Associated Psychological Services in Pasadena, California. Without the backdrop of their support there would be no book. I am grateful to Dr. Venema for reading many segments of manuscript and clarifying some things. Dr. Donald and Norma Tweedie read over some early efforts, and both urged me on. Dr. Tweedie is a professor at the Fuller Theological Seminary Graduate School of Psychology and is in independent practice. Mr. Edward Dayton, director of MARC (Missions Advanced Research and Communication Center) of World Vision International, rescued me from organizational disasters more than once. Besides being an excellent writer he has a keen mind and warm heart, the only kind of critic with whom I can do business. None of these people is responsible for whatever is not insightful or organized. I want to thank our children and some of their friends for their prayerful and consistent interest.

I owe much to that part of the body of Christ with whom I worship and grow in Christ and in relationships, Lake Avenue Congregational Church in Pasadena. My husband is one of the pastors, and our friends there have loved and cared for us for many years. To mention them all by name would take another chapter!

The first three chapters need to be read in succession, and the last two go together. Chapters 4 through 9 are intended to introduce an awareness of feelings in the areas under consideration in each, to start the reader on the path to personal discoveries of personal feelings about these subjects. I did not try to summarize them because there is no sense in which any of them is exhaustive. If they feel unfinished, it is because they are unfinished. With little effort, you will be able to add your own feeling experiences to each one. These six chapters are independent of each other and can be read in any order.

Where Feelings Fit In

1

You're a Christian husband. You know you're to love your wife as Christ loved the church. What do you do with your feelings of inadequacy, annoyance, exasperation? You don't have them?

You're a Christian wife. You understand you're to submit to your husband in everything. What do you do with your feelings of defensiveness, frustration, anger? You don't have them?

You're a Christian single person. You know that God will supply all your needs according to his riches in Jesus Christ. What do you do with your feelings of loneliness, dejection, longing? Perhaps you're a little more ready than your married brother or sister to admit such feelings if they're there.

You're a Christian. God is your loving heavenly Father. What do you do with feelings about him of doubt, distance, apathy? You're a living part of the body of Christ. For all the other members of his body you feel concern, acceptance, warmth. You don't? Then what do you do with your feelings of indifference, rejection, coldness?

You're a Christian. God has numbered the hairs of your head. You are valuable to him. How do you feel about yourself? Valued, worthwhile, acceptable?

Feelings came with Adam and Eve, and they're here to stay. God gave them to us. They're vital in the everyday business of living, yet most of us haven't given them careful, biblical thought.

There are many ways to approach our feelings. I intend to deal seriously with them, but I can't resist quoting from one of my favorite writers, George MacDonald, who pokes at them a bit.

> They had a feeling, or a feeling had them, till another feeling came and took its place. When a feeling was there, they felt as if it would never go; when it was gone they felt as if it had never been; when it returned, they felt as if it had never gone.[1]

Some will agree that this puts feelings in their proper place.

Two friends with analytical minds once discussed feelings with me. As each developed his train of thought it became obvious that feelings are complicated and can verge on the philosophical. I know the *experience* of feeling, but as I try to speculate on how feelings are involved, say, in the perception of beauty, or where feeling ends and the intellect takes over, I am overcome. Our fifteen-year-old daughter took a long walk on our vacation. "How was it?" I asked. "I walked and thought big thoughts," she said, "but they just mixed me up so I stopped."

This summer our family stood on the cliffs of Point Lobos, California. A man named Francis McComas called it "the greatest meeting of land and water in the world." The wind had molded the cypresses; the pounding sea, the smooth rock islands. The scene drove thought and feeling together. Such beauty didn't invite analysis; it called for sensing and praising God. My apprehension when our young son stood too close to the cliff's edge, my concern when an older son felt pain in a bad leg, the pleasure of watching the family search for sea life in tide pools down on the shore were graspable feelings. Those are the feelings discussed in this book, the feelings we can take hold of. Common, utilitarian feelings are the kind we want to pursue, the emotions of which we're aware, or can become aware, in the daily-ness of life.

The feelings I want to explore are our unsolicited, inner, personal reactions to life all around us. They come automatically from inside us as a response to something outside us.

Here are some things the feelings I'm working with are *not*. Feelings are not thoughts. Feelings are tied up with the part of our nervous system called the autonomic; thinking and reasoning involve the higher centers of our central nervous system. Ideally we can control our thinking, but our feelings are physiologically involved with our bodies in ways that aren't so manageable. We can, by thinking, decide to give a special gift to a friend, but it's harder to control the flush of pleasure as we give it. We can, by thinking, decide to make a confession, but we can't control the pounding of our heart while we're confessing. (An intriguing thing we'll discover is that when we aren't handling feelings well, our ability to think clearly is hampered.)

The feelings I'm talking about aren't physical ones, like the pain of a burn from a stove or the chill of a frosty morning. Our *responses* to physical sensations, the emotions, the inner experience of feeling, are what I want to consider.

Again, although feelings are real, they aren't reality itself. First, there is reality. Then, there is how we "see" or perceive reality. Finally, there is how we feel about what we perceive. For instance, a child brings home low grades on his report card. That is reality. I can see it as laziness or as the fault of an inadequate teacher or as something else. How do I feel about what I perceive? If I've perceived it as laziness, then I feel annoyed. If I've perceived it as poor teaching, then I feel sympathy for him.

Feelings can't be contained in any particular definition. One of the most obvious things about feelings, for example, is that they are felt. Yet, although feelings can be felt, although they "want" to be felt, it's possible not to feel them. They seem boundless in their extremes: big and little, earthly and fantastic, vital and incidental. They are like vises that grip, like vapors that vanish.

Why are feelings important to Christians? First, they are part of the dilemmas that accompany the "valleys" in our experience, valleys between the mountains of what we think we should be in Christ, our victory experiences. "Mountaintop experience" is a phrase in our Christian vocabulary we often use wistfully. Valleys and mountains are our way of describing the differences between how we behave and what we believe.

This morning I was stirred by the words of Peter as he begins his first letter. We have a living hope. A bright and lasting inheritance is waiting for us in heaven. Meanwhile through faith we are guarded by God's power. We are called to holy living. So, I should be conscious of that hope. The promise of eternity should be clearly in view. Faith should ward off Satan's fiery darts. Life should be lived in purity.

Only minutes after thinking about these things, I feel tempted to pursue an enticing wayward thought. I feel dull as I prepare lunch for guests. I feel irritated when I spill some rice. I feel frustrated after a phone call when it seems I've done very little to meet the need of a friend. These feelings rob me of my "spirituality."

Such mundane experiences in the midst of those glorious words of Peter illustrate what I want to say: there comes at least occasionally to every Christian, and very frequently to many, a deep desire to live on the mountaintop for God. Yet the daily-ness of life brings awareness of this gulf between the solid declarations of Scripture and our experience of them.

Can we be free from forever ascending and descending in our Christian experience? Our feelings seem to be a key to the baffling persistence of our valley/mountain living.

Second, feelings are integral to our humanity, and for many Christians being human is less than attractive. In our striving to work up to the mountaintop, to what we should become, our feelings remind us to our dismay that we are human. We haven't arrived. To admit our humanity, and the feelings and frailties that go with it, seems to deny our Christianity. To acknowledge and handle feelings honestly doesn't seem like a "spiritual" activity. In a recent address a speaker said, "Christians often behave as though they have resigned from the human race." But human is what God made us. Adam and Eve's innocent nakedness in the garden before the fall is symbolic of what we can now become. That is, we can have a kind of transparency that lets us live comfortably with ourselves and each other in our humanness. Our rescue by Jesus, our restoration, means that the more we become what we were at the beginning, the more like the way God made us, the better.

The way we handle our feelings helps us toward true humanity or keeps us from it. An honest attitude about our humanity will allow us to admit we have problems, even though problems of an inward sort haven't always been acceptable as part of the well-lived Christian life. They aren't mountaintop discussion material. (Thankfully, the climate is now changing in many churches.) Jesus said, "In the world you will have trouble." This follows all he has said in John 13, 14, 15, and 16, where he was speaking not only about problems from without but about inward pain and confusion as well. To have problems is not shameful.

When Christians are urged by pastors and teachers to live "supernaturally," I'm sure they mean that through God's power in us we should grow more like Jesus, have his wisdom in decisions and in relationships, and have optimism and courage and discipline in the face of a decaying world. But many Christians interpret this to mean we must be superhuman, and as they try to live at a super level they're forced to battle the reality of inward problems. They can't take care of the problems because they have to pretend they aren't there. Sometimes we can even fool ourselves into thinking we have no problems, but our ostrich behavior doesn't fool many other people. Something about us doesn't ring true.

When we don't handle problems realistically, we have scarcely entered into the process of becoming whole. Sadly, when Christians do become honest inside, they often resign themselves to the idea that they aren't up to "true spirituality" after all, and feel a kind of defeat.

God made us in his image, but he understands and accepts us marred and scarred. He understands and accepts our human framework of his image. The final victory of deliverance from our fallenness, the becoming altogether what God made us to be, is hardly in sight. It is future tense. We have been bought by Jesus for a future hope, but meanwhile it's OK to be "on the way"—with all that being human involves.

In accepting ourselves as God made us, we find feelings a part of our life; and because God gave them to us, they are of worth. John Fischer sings:

> Don't you know I'm human?
> That means I have to feel
> All the things a human feels
> Although the Lord is real....*

Third, Christians are often encouraged to look "up and out," but they aren't taught to look in, where our feelings are. On the face of it, this seems right. The best is God, and he is "up." Others are next most important, and they are "out." I am least worthy of attention and inspection. There is nothing to gain by looking in. It isn't too nice in there.

Now consider these basic theological truths: God thought I was so valuable that he became a human so I could know him. In Christ, God died so that I would always be alive.

God chose to live in me. What's in me is worth taking care of, because by word and deed God has declared me worthwhile. C. S. Lewis has Screwtape, an undersecretary to the devil, say about God, "He has a curious fantasy of making all these disgusting little human vermin into what He calls his 'free' lovers and servants—'sons' is the word He uses."[2]

To know ourselves is essential. Peter begins his first letter by saying, "You have been born anew..." and "Like newborn babes...." Our second birth is the key to the rightness of looking inward. The question of Nicodemus shows that to that learned and distinguished man the inward look was somewhat alien: "Can a man enter a second time into his mother's womb and be born?" In no way can we become squirming, blinking, tiny pieces of tender-skinned humanity. It's *inside* that the new birth has come. It's inside that we learn to love, become pure, and cease objectionable actions.

And how are all these inside things to happen unless we're looking inside to be partners with God in their happening? How can I ask God, "Search me and know my thoughts, try me and see if there is any wicked way in me" unless I'm searching with him in the process? If I refuse to look inside, how can he do his work in there? Unless we look inward, how are we to work out our own salvation with fear and trembling? Certainly not by looking at other Christians, trying to stick newness on the outside, or even by looking only at Jesus. We are more often invited in Scripture to *come* to him.

To know ourselves is to know our feelings. Without the inward look we can know Scripture but "apply" it only like a mustard plaster. That's what the Pharisees tried to do by binding Scripture on their foreheads. I'm certainly no stranger to the kind of "application" that never gets past the barriers to the heart. Yet it's impossible to search myself honestly without running head-on into things I don't like, including "bad" feelings.

Where Feelings Fit In

The ways people come to Christ are different, but almost all involve some sense of need. I have a friend who met the Lord simply because the gospel makes good sense, but such a person is unusual. People realize they're needy, accept the fact that they are, and then become open to change. Those who are open to Jesus Christ and the change he brings are "born again."

But the same principle applies to people who already know God. Once we've become Christians, more change can come only as we keep accepting what we are inside. Psychologist Carl Rogers stated that people change only when they are aware of where they are in the present and then accept themselves. He said of himself, "... the curious paradox is that when I accept myself as I am, then I change."[3] Christians tend to be so dissatisfied and burdened with themselves, ashamed of their imperfection. There is nothing Christ-like in this attitude. The Holy Spirit longs for us to accept the overwhelming advantage we have in this adventure of changing: the fact that he is inside us, with us, loving us inside.

Jesus and I both know that ugly things are in me. He said, and I experience, that "out of the heart come evil thoughts, murder, adultery, fornication, theft, false witness, slander." But what else did Jesus say? "My yoke is easy and my burden is light." Any of his dedicated servants knows he isn't talking about the old rocking chair in the cool of the evening. He's talking about what goes on *inside* in our life with him, including the way we feel about ourselves.

He wants us to be lighthearted about ourselves inside. His forgiveness of sin is immediate; unforgiven sins are the only burdens we need to bear in our life with ourselves. The burdens of others, the pain of others, even the sufferings we experience are another matter.

God accepts me as I am, inside, now. Why shouldn't I accept myself whatever my feelings? He loved me before he saved me. He loves, he *likes*, me the way I am. Through his example I learn what love is. The Holy Spirit can fill me more when I'm not struggling with regrets about what I am or am not. With honest self-accepting appraisal, I can begin to see God more clearly. Honesty becomes not only a virtue, but a relief, a blessing. I can be honest with myself about myself; I can feel at home with me. My feelings are the channel to knowing myself.

Part of the easy yoke, the light burden, is being your own friend. The things you feel for, long for, or enjoy in a friend could well be directed to yourself. You want to feel your friend is accepting, caring for you just the way you are, interested in your well-being. Nothing cools friendship so quickly as failure to be in touch with joys and sorrows, or being judgmental. Nothing will more surely cause inner conflict than failure to relate genuinely to yourself, to be your own good friend.

If we're comfortable about ourselves, it's easier to accept other people as they are. We no longer need to build ourselves up by criticizing others. We no longer are threatened and insecure when confronted with views and ideas different from our own. When I consider that I am a human creation of God and nothing more (but nothing less), then I no longer need to expect perfection in myself. Not needing to be perfect, I no longer am a slave to comparisons with others.

To feel good inside about myself is to be free from dependence on events or relationships or possessions for happiness. I can be shattered if something goes wrong with any of those things when I depend on them.

So, where do feelings fit into the life of a Christian? We begin to discover a leveling-off place between our mountain and valley experiences when we allow all of our humanity to become a respected part of us. We make progress in the process of being all God intended for us when our feelings, an integral part of humanity, become acceptable to us as well. The love of God doesn't change because we've begun to discover what we're like inside. Because God loves us we can be free to care for ourselves, to admit honestly how we feel. And we find that acceptance of others grows with acceptance of self.

Our feelings are important to our Christian growth. Let's discuss our feelings. Let's consider human wholeness and health. Let's exult in being human children of God.

Notes

1. C. S. Lewis, *George MacDonald: An Anthology* (London: Geoffrey Bles, 1946) #351, p. 123.

2. C. S. Lewis, *Screwtape Letters* (New York: Macmillan, 1948) p. 17.

3. Carl Rogers, *On Becoming a Person* (Boston: Houghton Mifflin, 1970) p. 17.

Feelings Are Friends

2

Feelings are as common as breathing, as useful as the utensils in my kitchen, as rich as Fort Knox, as varied as the flowers in gardens, as spectacular as fireworks on the Fourth, as annoying as a flat tire, as awful as an earthquake. What a shame so many Christians have colored them yellow-brownish-gray and stuffed them in storage. God built feelings into us for growth, maturity, fulfillment. They need fresh air. We think that opening the closet door is risky. We get alarmed because feelings seem hard to handle. We get caught in the "battered feelings" syndrome.

Why do Christians batter their feelings? Even if we come to the place where we're ready to listen to what's happening inside us, why do we have this grudge against feelings? One reason may be a response to our culture. When we see people "do their thing," follow the dictates of their feelings, we see them as contributing to society's problems. If feelings lead people into destructive activity, the less attention we give them the better.

Another reason we're wary of feelings is that we suspect they're unreliable. We find them fickle and flighty. They lift us up and let us down. Highs don't last and lows are painful. We think that growing spiritually is a matter of climbing steadily upward, getting better and better, and we can't rely on anything as unstable as feelings to get us to the top.

Then again there are the times of crisis when we move our bodies and minds to meet emergencies. Feelings seem immaterial. We behave well and we suppose it didn't take feelings to do it.

The main reason we can't look squarely at our feelings is that they help us see our real "self," and we don't like what we see. If we free our feelings to be felt, they just add to our age-old tendency to be disappointed with ourselves. So often they're "bad": anger, envy, suspicion, the emotions of temptation, the vague uneasiness that grips us from time to time. We've been told that Christians have been lifted up out of all that. If anyone knew what bad things are going on inside us, we would be found "unspiritual." The result is that we spend a great deal of energy keeping feelings in storage so we won't have to worry about what others think. We sit in self-judgment as well.

Although we generally aren't afraid of "good" feelings (they fit in with being good Christians), we sometimes have trouble even with them. Too much joy is a little odd, perhaps even thoughtless. A friend recently told me that her life is so satisfying she deliberately tries to play her joy down for fear of adding to the depression of not-so-happy people around her.

We play surgical games with our feelings when they're negative. We cut away at ourselves when we're angry or hurt, doing quick "exploratories" and closing up the wounds because we don't know what to do with our emotional cancers. We treat our feelings as we do persistent children when we're busy. We try to shake them off or shush them up. Either we can't afford the time to deal with them properly, or we don't know how. Poor handling of feelings quickly becomes habitual.

Negative and positive feelings aren't bad or good. *Feelings are morally neutral.* It's what we do with them that involves being bad or good, being sinful or righteous. There is nothing wrong with bad feelings—Jesus certainly had them when he cleansed the temple, at Gethsemane, on the cross, and in other instances, and he never sinned.

Jesus' anger burned while he whipped at the tables of the money changers and drove the livestock from his Father's house. At Gethsemane Jesus felt fear and terror at the prospect before him. Only the exhausting depth of an unfathomable emotional struggle could account for "sweat ... like great drops of blood." On the cross Jesus experienced crushing despair and rejection, the incomprehensible emotional agony of his Father's absence.

Anger, terror, despair. Our Savior wasn't a robot programmed to do a certain job on earth. He was a feeling human being who constantly had to decide to do his Father's will, and who experienced all of our human struggle with feelings. His habits of *handling* his feelings were built into his thinking, and they never betrayed him. One reason he was so whole is that he always knew what was going on inside. Look for this integration in Jesus when you read the Gospels.

We handle our negative feelings in a number of ways. Sometimes people who think they have negative feelings under control have buried them. "We do not bury our emotions *dead;* they remain *alive...*"[1] But consciously they are forgotten. What has really happened is that in the process of actively rejecting feelings we do not like, we have pushed them back into our minds until they have dropped out of sight, out of "feel," into the deep abyss of the subconscious. But the damage is done. Fresh experiences bring new "bad" feelings, which, when handled the same way, simply add to the load.

Sooner or later, because the buried emotions are still alive, the difficulty will be too much to handle. Our personalities are poisoned. Our negative feelings rise up to create a disturbance. Depression grips us, for example, even in the midst of the fellowship of believers. These depressed states refuse to be treated with a cup of coffee in a quiet restaurant or a couple of hours with a good book or even a comforting assurance that "Jesus is the answer."

The term *depression* is like an umbrella to cover the most common difficulties that buried feelings produce. Life lacks sparkle, everything seems dull. We have a sense of hopelessness, an almost unrelieved case of blahs. We no longer have happy and satisfying contacts with other people, even while contacts with others provide the only source of relief. When we are alone or going about our daily responsibilities, we experience a steady low. Depression affects our appetite for food, our sexual responses, the level of our physical energies, our sleeping habits.

A second thing we do with bad feelings is no better. We dismiss them to the back of our minds where they simmer away. Yet they refuse to disappear. We know they're in the background. For Christians this can lead to spiritual dishonesty. We stick to acceptable patterns of Christian activity and conversation, but we aren't genuine. Sometimes we try to cover these feelings with extra enthusiasm, but inside the unreality is still there. Something is missing in our relationship with God and other believers. We just don't feel *good* about being Christian. Sometimes we see the shocking phenomenon of a pillar of the church suddenly launching into a divorce because he or she has finally concluded that everything is just not worth the internal agony.

To become involved in some satisfying activity outside the church fellowship may not seem completely acceptable. So, for fear of upsettting a spouse, or having to face the criticism or condemnation of fellow believers, a person settles for dishonesty—and the quiet disillusionment goes on and on. It takes courage to buck the status quo, to be vulnerable, to admit need and seek help in this dual role.

We need to accept our negative feelings and not bury them or push them back. They should be accepted along with positive feelings, for as we grow in Christ they all have a God-given role to play. Negative feelings are like ther-mometers. They can warn us that all is not well. They are helpful signs that point to danger. They need to be watched. Temptations to sin are powerful precisely *because* they're loaded with feelings. How good to be aware of these emotions. How alarming if they aren't there.

The tragic thing about burying or smothering negative feelings is that it doesn't stop with them. The good, positive ones get clobbered at the same time. We don't have a built-in, automatic sorting machine that lets our positive feelings out genuinely while our negative ones are kept bottled up; false cheer is a sad thing. Peace, confidence, optimism, happy alertness to life, the ability to live on the growing edge, the desire to love and be loved, courage, enthusiasm, active empathy toward others: all are robbed of the atmosphere they need to be fruitful, a "freed-up" personality.

Feelings are like antennae. We need to be sensitive if we're to have healthy relationships. We can learn to approach others with a thoughtfulness born of knowing how we want to be treated. Feelings let us know when relationships are in trouble and need to be mended. In the body of Christ we are put together by God with many people who aren't like ourselves, but to whom we're committed for eternity. When we don't feel good about someone, that feeling can signal the need for the thoughtful building of a relationship.

Well-trained feelings can be reliable servants. We need to treat them with respect and at the same time to be aware of their status, so they don't become like servants who ingratiate themselves into positions of power. We can't trust them to serve us if we don't know what they're doing. A friend recently told me how she began to snap at her husband and daughter when her father became seriously ill. Unreasonable expressions of anger toward others result when feelings are masters, not servants. Sincere and complete apologies can ease but seldom erase such unmastered outbursts. Feelings can serve us faithfully through times of crisis. Those who do handle emergencies and difficulties best are those in touch with their feelings.

For the Christian, feelings are simple tools that anyone can use to grow in faith. For many Christians they've become rusty and all but useless through neglect. Tools go a long way toward lightening life's load. They're a kind of extension of ourselves by which things get done, but they're not the substance or the stuff we're working with. They're the scissors but not the cloth.

Feelings aren't the quiet, searching, learning times with God. They aren't the relationships with all the people our lives touch. They aren't the outreach into the world taking us into all kinds of situations. They aren't the reality, but they are tools with which we work with reality.

Feelings need to be separated from the facts or substance of life, so they can be handled. Unless this happens, they are ruling where they have no right. Unless we're handling them well they seem to have a life of their own that we can't manage, some strength that makes us dependent on them. When we've learned to take care of our feelings, we have conscious and comfortable control of them. We have them in our grasp. The more we work with them, the more we appreciate them.

As we grow to know God and ourselves better, as our feelings become keen-edged tools, "feeling good" can even become synonymous with being in God's will. But few of us have learned to be in touch with ourselves, to handle our feelings well enough to be acquainted with this wonderful state of affairs.

Feelings are intertwined with our bodies and minds and spirits. Dr. Paul Tournier, a physician, was led by God to abandon a lucrative medical practice in order to spend more time with fewer people. He recognized the impact that the problems of life have on the human body. His books emphasize how much feelings affect our physical well-being. A man distressed over disturbed relationships in his life told me that as a result of distress he had become a careless driver. Even a headache distracts most of us from "enjoying" God. We feel most "spiritual" when life goes smoothly. For years a friend of mine had actue diarrhea every Sunday morning. The difficulty stopped when she realized its cause: emotional upheaval she had experienced as a child forced to attend a church she hated. So we are continually faced with our complex unity as persons, and feelings are woven through this complicated fabric.

It pays to examine our feelings as a legitimate activity. Emotions are a potent force for whole or fragmented lives. Poor treatment of our feelings is at the root of many unfortunate decisions, twisted relationships, and all the ensuing complications.

Feelings have too often become disdained: feared, maligned, disparaged, neglected. We haven't looked carefully at Jesus, we haven't entered thoughtfully into his life or we'd have become aware of the negative feelings of his humanity. Whatever he experienced, we can experience without sin. We are called to be like him, and one part of the process is to learn the useful, tool-like character of all our feelings. The sooner we begin to live sensibly with them, the sooner they will be what God intended them to be, friends and not foes.

Notes

1. John Powell, *Why Am I Afraid to Tell You Who I Am?* Argus Communications, Chicago, Ill., p. 75.

Our Need to Handle Feelings 3

My husband and I are spending a relaxing day near a marina. From the window we can see a few of the thousands of boats docked in several inlets. Each boat fits snugly next to its neighbor in its prescribed slot. How unlike feelings! How difficult to handle them in ways that will moor us securely to the dock like these boats. How nice it would be to have our own niche, protected from storms and dangers, where we can bob gently with tides that come and go so quietly we hardly notice them. It might be boring at times but it would certainly be a relief in our hurting and weary world. We would scarcely be feeling at all. "Answers" to how to handle feelings would be unnecessary.

But that isn't the case, is it? We're out in mid-ocean—though not Jean-Paul Sartre's shoreless ocean, and not without oars or compass. Nor are we alone in our little boats. We have to handle our feelings well to be good sailors in all kinds of weather, including the choppy seas and unavoidable storms.

It's characteristic of Christians that we follow trends in our culture, always lagging behind but nevertheless following. Now our culture is becoming increasingly ready to live by feelings. We in the church will too, but *our* call is to handle them well.

The way God intended for feelings to be used is basically simple. Yet what should be an almost unconscious process of healthy integration of feelings is far from common among us. Rather than battering or smothering or burying our feelings, we have to relearn that God-intended simplicity. We must change ingrained habits, which takes time. Changing also involves willingness to be uncomfortable. We begin to change first by listening to feelings, second by acknowledging and accepting them for what they are, and then by choosing a way to work them out.

Listening is the first and probably most challenging step in the process of handling feelings well, especially if we aren't used to listening. It's a matter of hearing what goes on inside, particularly those things that we find disturbing. When something has just happened, it may be easy to identify what you're feeling—provided you've moved past the idea that negative feelings are sinful in themselves. But if something happened a few hours ago, already you may have begun to take care of it in your habitual way: burying it (actively pushing it away from you, probably without realizing it), or suppressing it (telling yourself it isn't important), instead of working it through (if you've learned to do this). If it happened a long time ago, and it's gone from your consciousness, it will take longer to hear it. It may be one big bad thing that you've buried. It may be a thousand little ones. Of course many negative feelings and the experiences that caused them are beyond recall. Identify what you can. You may need to listen beyond any ''good'' feelings you've used to cover up more honest feelings that aren't pleasant.

Do you have a relationship with someone in which there's a lack of peace? Is there someone you don't feel good about? Is there an experience with someone that still hurts? Deep down do you resent someone? Has someone disagreed with you, and it still rankles inside? Is there a person significant to you with whom you feel unaccepted or insecure? Do you feel uncomfortable around someone whose doctrines about God and the church are different from yours? When bad feelings are closest to home, we may be most reluctant to identify them, but angers and hurts poison family members against each other. We make jokes about in-laws. Perhaps this acceptable habit has made our negative feelings about them easier to "hear." Is it possible that you resent your wife, husband, brother, sister? Listen. If you've identified someone and an associated hurt, is there something just underneath that feeling that more closely describes it? Are you jealous, disappointed, embarrassed? Have you felt rejected?

Recently I realized that I didn't feel good about someone. I identified the feeling as resentment. But why did I resent that person? It took more inner listening to realize that I'd sensed rejection when I'd shared something that hadn't been well received. It had happened months ago. I had come away feeling confused. I hadn't "heard" what was just underneath. The original hurt was still there, although I had tried to forget it.

How about temptation? Listening carefully to our feelings can help us deal with temptation before it leads to sin. These emotions need to be heard quickly. Scripture gives us three specific pieces of information about temptation:

(1) "Let no one say when he is tempted, 'I am tempted by God' " (James 1:12);

(2) Jesus was "in every respect tempted as we are, yet without sinning" (Hebrews 4:15); and

(3) there is a "way of escape," so that we'll be able to handle the heaviest temptations when they come (1 Corinthians 10:13).

So, let no one say that he or she isn't tempted. Everyone is tempted. Satan has done his work well when he has led a believer past temptation into sin. If you believe you're beyond temptation, perhaps you think that the feelings of temptation are themselves sinful, and you haven't been willing to listen to them. Such thinking lives next door to smugness and pride. If temptation is no problem to you, maybe you've let some particular temptation lead into a sinful act so often that it no longer bothers you. If you're a confirmed gossip, Satan is likely satisfied with that; no need to lead you into adultery. Gossip seems like such a minor sin, doesn't it? Satan will settle for that, or for anything that becomes careless and habitual sinning. Dr. Robert Munger of Fuller Theological Seminary remarked that "sin carries with it its own anesthetic." Being in touch with feelings is the key to awakening from this stupor and being delivered from it.

Success in overcoming temptation begins with listening to and recognizing feelings. Feelings of temptation, whether small and subtle or overwhelming or burdensome, are always powerful because they're enticing. Their attractiveness makes us want to play with them, so they find hospitality in our thoughts. Sam Shoemaker suggested that "most of our basic instincts revolve around money, sex, and power... What gets our emotions usually gets us."[1] Each of these areas is loaded with disaster potential.

What about your feelings toward God? How do you really feel about him? Do you secretly feel he has failed you? Are you bitter toward him? The perplexity or dismay or anger you may feel against God has come from some experience. Identify it. Why are your feelings about God not good? In what ways are you fooling yourself about the success of your Christian experience? Is it all you say it is? Are your "Praise Gods" and "Hallelujahs" genuine?

Our positive feelings also need a hearing. They're so easily drowned by today's weary voices of gloom and resignation. Has someone contributed something to your life? Has someone encouraged you? Have you felt concern for someone else? Who are those you feel best about and why? Are you comforted? interested? proud? inspired? grateful? Have you expressed these kinds of positive feelings to those around you? Delight and optimism, sympathy and approval, anticipation and daring, are all feelings. They are the spice of life. There is no way to benefit from them fully unless we're listening to all our feelings.

Listen. What is it you're feeling? Sometimes when we're listening, the feeling-voices don't come steadily in connected succession. We need quietness, a good atmosphere for hearing what goes on inside our lives. Most of us can't find time for long silences. But even in the midst of the busyness of everyday living you can feel if something isn't in tune in your life and begin to listen. Suddenly, hours or even days later, you'll hear what you're waiting for, like recalling the name of someone you've "misplaced" or a melody you'd forgotten.

Listening to feelings can become a painful process from which it's easy to back away. To listen calls for patience, persistence, even courage. You may need some comfortable, knowledgeable person to listen to you while you listen to yourself—a friend, pastor, professional counselor. But in an atmosphere of quiet acceptance of self, given time to think alone, most people can make significant progress by themselves. Barry Stevens has written interestingly about being her own therapist.[2] The Christian has the presence of the Holy Spirit to assist in this inner exploration. If you can explore with a sense of adventure, without judging yourself when a negative feeling emerges, without backing away from the process, you'll learn to hear what is going on inside. Scripture will help. Romans 8:1 says, "There is therefore now no condemnation for those who are in Christ Jesus," and 8:31-39 is an enlargement of that fact. We can listen to ourselves without fear.

After you've taken this first giant step of *listening and recognizing,* the second step in handling feelings is to *acknowledge* what you've discovered about them. You need to admit and accept what is going on inside. Because of our dislike of negative feelings, this also may be painful. You may feel hate, anger, jealousy, or insecurity in your place in the body of Christ (Do people *really* love me?). In addition to feelings there may be some uncovered facts: an unforgiving heart, an unforgiven hurt.

Whatever it is that has caused you to feel bad, acknowledge it. There it is. It belongs to you and no one else. Put it out in front of you and look at it. Look at that hurting thing, that bunch of bad feelings. Probably you didn't ask for that load, but it's all yours. God sees it. You and God are looking at it together. How does God feel about it? J. B. Phillips translates 1 Peter 5:7, "You can throw the whole weight of your anxieties upon him, for you are his personal concern." God cares. He cares that you're hurting. He cares about the people you've hurt. He loves you with the feelings out there in front of you just as much as he did when they were inside and not admitted. When we're accustomed to listening (recognizing) and acknowledging (admitting), these become a single step.

The third step in handling feelings is to decide what you'll do with the discoveries you've made. It's decision time. Committed Christians certainly don't have to be told that to follow feelings and do whatever emotions say may get us into trouble. Christian behavior calls for thinking things over. Often there's nothing at all that you need to do, or can do, about past hurts and angers and feelings of failure. But the time of acknowledgment can be turned into a time of prayer and recommitment. There may be need for confession to God or to some other person. You may need to forgive. And you may need to be careful and sensitive when you share with others your feelings of temptation. At this point especially, honesty must be coupled with discernment.

When we've recognized and admitted negative feelings, there are options from which to choose. When we've come to grips with these feelings, we have a base from which to be decisive, to choose to do what God wants rather than to bungle along. We need to know God well in order to do this, so we need to know the Scripture well.

We make good decisions when we try to inform ourselves fully about what is happening inside and about what God wants of us. Decisions are not to be hurried or unwise, but thoughtfully considered. On the other hand, decision-making in general takes less time as we get used to this way of doing it. When you're up-to-date in this kind of deciding process, choosing a path of action isn't difficult, although living it out, carrying it through, can be hard.

Not long ago, my husband was recovering from a heart attack. I was feeling pleased about bringing him home from the hospital. At the same time, I was confronted with a coming election in our community in which I knew I would have to take a stand unpopular with many close friends. I'm not a born crusader, and this problem came down on me like an avalanche. A year before, confusion and depression would have covered me quickly and consciously. Now, in better touch with my feelings, I "heard" anger. I was angry about two things I could identify: the first was intrusion of an unpleasant matter into our personal lives at that particular time; the second was the conflict I anticipated in relationships with friends over the election. I handled the first by sharing it with a friend and praying about it. Then I was able to wait for a good time to talk it over with my husband. Handling the second anger made it necessary to think through what I would do, what action to take in the weeks ahead. Weeks later, I found I had taken much the same action I did years before in a similar election; but this time, although I was still sensitive and caring about relationships, I wasn't at war with myself as I'd been before. I felt peaceful because I did what I thought was the right thing to do.

When we haven't listened and admitted, it's easy to put our angers and other negative feelings on someone else. Recently a woman was describing the unreasonableness of her boss. "He must have made you very angry," I said. Her reply was "No, I'm not angry. It's just disgusting." Her supervisor's behavior was enough to justify anger. If she could have acknowledged that feeling, she wouldn't have been forced to enter into the judgment that disgust always calls for.

Jesus met a challenging situation in a different way. In Mark 3:1-6 Jesus healed a man on the sabbath, and his accusers were there to condemn him for this good act. "And he looked around at them with anger, grieved at their hardness of heart." Here he handled anger by turning it into grief that he himself had to bear. He chose not to poison his relationships further, even with those whose dislike of him was fast turning into unreasonable hatred.

The power of temptation begins to fade when we've heard and accepted the feelings that are involved. A further step, a decision, can deliver us out of enemy territory in that particular skirmish or battle. A friend with whom we can share our rock-bottom feelings at a time of heavy temptation is a special gift from God. I believe there is someone in the body of Christ for every person to have as this kind of friend. But sharing our temptations with even the closest friend seems so humiliating that many aren't willing to do it. More threatening is the fear that even a good friend can bear only so much; there is risk involved. Yet the uglier and heavier the temptation, the more we need to share it.

Remember, we aren't less spiritual when we've been tempted. Jesus' own struggles in the wilderness and at Gethsemane were acute, but not sinful. Talk your struggle over with God, involve yourself in some rewarding activity. One course of action is to act out your temptation in your mind to the ultimate outcome of what it is you're tempted to do. That can be so unpleasant if you care about the feelings of people that the temptation quickly loses its sparkle.

Having shoved negative feelings aside in my own life over a long period of time, I rejoice in the clean air of feelings recognized and acknowledged and decisions reached with more ease and conviction. But I find there's a price to pay for becoming feeling-oriented. As we become feeling-aware we feel more pain in ourselves and in other people. It hurts to live in touch with pain, but there is beauty in the identification with people that this brings.

There is no question that the freshness of living in the moment, handling feelings well, is part of the "more abundant life." Positive feelings are heightened and steadied. Joy is more sustained when we're freed from emotional blocks that pull us down. As the valleys are lifted there is a sense in which the mountains are leveled; our happiness isn't unstable or "mountaintop." It is independent, at least to some extent, of what is going on outside ourselves.

For most of us, what is going on outside ourselves challenges us to the core. A resourceful and well-adjusted friend recently said, "I'm as stretched now as I can be and still cope." Christians will become increasingly sensitive to a hurting world, increasingly called upon to bear burdens. We had better be able to handle ourselves well. Since our behavior is significantly determined by how we manage our emotions, we had better learn to handle them well. We must listen to and accept our feelings, and then seriously consider them in deciding how we will behave. The next six chapters are intended to stir our thinking about feelings; they will begin to help us become "feeling" aware. Chapter 10 will enlarge the three steps in handling feelings.

The last time our daughter came home from college she brought me a poster of a water pump going full blast. Underneath, it read, "Feelings are not like faucets you can turn on and off." That's right. But you can decide how the water will be used. You can learn to handle feelings.

Notes

1. Sam Shoemaker, *The Experiment of Faith: A Handbook for Beginners* (N. Y., Harper & Bros. Publishers, 1957) p. 23.

2. Carl R. Rogers & Barry Stevens, *Person to Person: The Problem of Being Human* (Moab, Utah: Real People Press, 1967), p. xiii.

Feelings and God 4

Omniscient, omnipresent, omnipotent. I like those words about God because they're the biggest ones I know to describe him. But to write them reinforces my conviction that language is so unlike the thing it tries to express; it's so limited— little marks of ink on paper. God is all-knowing, everywhere-present, all-powerful. We affirm a God whose love is ocean-deep, then experience him as if we're scrunched up in a small bathtub.

Before we hike down to the valleys and up on the hills of daily relationship to him, it's good to remember that he is wholly Other, complete in himself, sovereign in human affairs. I remember bursts of amazement when I first began to know him. What came through to me was the remarkable practicality, the inherent workableness, of his plan. It was mysterious and incomprehensible, but also sensible and graspable, within the capacity of any human being. We have a "Shepherd's Class" for the mentally retarded in our church. They understand the love of Jesus. So do members of Cal Tech Christian Fellowship, about seventy-five highly intelligent students at nearby California Institute of Technology.

What a God we have! God the Father, in compassion communicating to us and, fatherlike, available. God the

Son, willing to leave equality with the Father to come to his own creation, clothing himself in the dust of humanity to accomplish his saving work. God the Holy Spirit, living in us, underneath us, above us, around us, comforting, guiding, teaching.

Of all the gaps in our lives, "getting it together" with God everyday seems to be the most difficult one for Christians to bridge. Feeling comfortable and at home with him doesn't seem to be a common experience. If non-Christians are uncomfortable in his presence, that's a good sign. It shows they're aware that he is there and that somehow they aren't on the right footing with him. But if his children are uncomfortable with him, it's another matter. Our confession and his forgiveness of specific sins are essential to a feeling of well-being with God. But even after confession and forgiveness, many have never been happy with him; I think they never expect to be.

Earnest Christians are convinced that God proved his love for us at the cross. Only once in awhile do most Christians experience feelings in response to his love—relief, satisfaction, tenderness, affection, joy, courage, zest for his work, security even when his hand is heavy. Instead we often feel false guilt, disappointment, coolness, emptiness. A satisfying matching of ourselves with God is a tender thing and is based on God's love: the way God feels about us and the way he has acted toward us. God has never sat indifferent in the heavens. We forget that he loved us with his feelings before he sent his Son to die for us.

Since our relationship with God is the most important one of all, more significant than our relationship with any other person, it's the area where we've been given the most opinions, suggestions, formulas, definitions, encouragements, criticisms, and judgments. We need all the help we can get, but difficulty comes when we're unable to digest all the "spiritual" food that comes to us. Faith is of course not a feeling; but *how* we experience God, including how we feel about him, significantly affects our faith. Feelings influence our "objective" perception of the great Source of faith. Why are we uncomfortable with God?

One reason is that in our minds we evaluate God's attitude toward us on the basis of our performance. He has acted magnificently toward us; we like to think we must make even a shadowy effort to act like him. No matter how often we mouth the phrase that we're "saved by faith," no matter how often we solemnly verbalize that we're saved and "kept" by him alone, no matter how adequately we've grasped that intellectually, our feelings haven't caught up. We aren't feeling comfortable because whatever we have done, or are, isn't good enough.

As I learned about feelings I realized that my sense of God's presence was diminished when I felt inadequate and unacceptable. When I became aware of what acceptance is, I realized that God totally accepts his children *where we are,* all the time. The things in my life that *I* couldn't accept I felt he couldn't accept either, and I had to try to meet him over or around these unacceptable things. Only in looking back do I realize what was happening. When it was happening, our relationship suffered a kind of confusion. Now, it works for me just to say honestly to him, at any time, "Here is where I am, Lord. I am undone over this situation, or this person." Sometimes I don't even say "over this sin," because he knows it's imperfection in me and I know it too.

It isn't only that I've broken some specific command for which he forgives me. My creaturehood is an inescapable fact. I am so unlike him, so human. C. S. Lewis said the "sheer difference" between us and God "is one compared with which the difference between an archangel and a worm is quite insignificant."[1] My unworthiness is obvious to us both. I think of this when we sing,

> "Jesus, Thy blood and righteousness
> My beauty are, my glorious dress."

When I'm most conscious of my need, I've only begun to be conscious of it. When I think I'm no longer pretending, I've only started taking off the masks. The important thing is to become comfortable in his presence while remembering whose presence it is. If I'm not "at home" with him, we can't do business together.

I think of a boy in kindergarten where I helped for awhile. He was "culturally deprived." He had a speech impediment. God had made his skin dark. He would start on a project fairly happily and soon disaster would begin to overtake his efforts. He would push the work aside, tears would come to the surface, and with his mouth twisted he'd say, "Aw, I've messed up again." And so have I. I've messed up again and again, but it hasn't worn God down a bit. He lets me make mistakes. I can live fully in each moment. I can use the word *existential* without shivering.

A second reason for our lack of feeling comfortable with God comes from being fed untrue doctrines about him from childhood. Bad feelings about God have been worked into our very being. What we learn intellectually about him in our earliest years immediately colors our feelings about him and affects us all our lives. Some of us learn bad things. A relative of mine was taught as a child that God is the "All-Seeing Eye," and her predominant mental picture for years was a Great Eye following her everywhere. No need to comment on the feelings involved.

Thousands, raised in the doctrinal atmosphere that one can lose one's salvation through not living up to certain standards of behavior, have known fearful feelings of insecurity: a "loving God" can turn away if my behavior doesn't meet some set of expectations. As my husband and I have talked with such people over the years, we've found this teaching almost impossible to overcome. It's different from the warnings in Scripture about being careful in what we do to live lives worthy of the gospel of Christ. Feelings connected with a touchy and capricious God are never feelings of comfort and cheer.

In certain areas our discomfort with God comes into sharp focus. One is when our "quiet times" or "personal devotions" seem to go dry, when trying to spend time concentrating on God is more of a struggle than a blessing. We can be far too harsh on ourselves and on each other, trying to promote this personal, intimate interaction with the One who loves us so much. We can be guilt-ridden over our failure to spend time with him. Or we rationalize our failure, thinking he loves us so much and is so big that our being "with him" in this special sense doesn't really matter.

We can become judgmental, evaluating other believers on the basis of their time spent with God and the Bible. Often people who are vocally most concerned about the spiritual progress of others are themselves threatened and insecure. To nail someone for lack of "time spent in the Word" must make the accuser feel more spiritual. For such a person, could it be that deep down there's a sort of twisted comfort that someone else isn't doing too well with God? If being with God doesn't feel good, then we'll avoid making the effort. No amount of *telling* the necessity of a quiet time to a person caught in this web of negative feelings will help.

All of my Christian life I have believed in eternal security, but for a long time I didn't believe in twenty-four-hour security. If I hadn't deliberately spent time recognizing God and giving him my day, I couldn't be sure he had control of it. I've come to realize what it was that often made my quiet times unsatisfactory, even though my intention was always to worship, to get guidance, to intercede. When warm feelings of anticipation about being with God are absent, only good intentions will make us try to spend a time alone with him. And good intentions are often weak motivators when the crunch comes.

Since God is outside of time and it isn't morning, noon, or night with him, any time at all will do. And since there are no days or hours with him, only an eternal Now, we don't need to get tied up in knots if somehow in our twenty-four hours we've missed a meeting. I think there must be a personal "quiet time" equivalent of the fact that "the sabbath was made for man, not man for the sabbath." We are the losers if we don't take advantage of time to be with him, but we don't need to feel guilty if we haven't clocked in at some special time.

Over the years my personal choice of the best time was early morning. Unfortunately the perspective of a new day didn't erase my problems and the feelings that went with them. Many times I would direct my attention to the Lord, Bible in hand and a plan to go with it. I knew good approaches to the Bible, and I knew the difference between intellectualizing Scripture and making it personal. The "feeling" problems crowded in anyway. A troubled relationship or the needs of our children would grip me. *Something* didn't jell in the rarified atmosphere that I thought should typify time spent with God. Heavy pleading consistently characterized those times. I was at the meeting only because I wanted something from the only One who could grant it. After a few minutes I would grab at a thought from some verse and give it up to wait for a better hour.

I've learned that whenever I'm kept from having satisfaction in devotional ventures with God, it's because I haven't taken him with me where I am. I've simply tried to elevate myself to some height that I couldn't reach. I couldn't bring my feelings to match my knowledge of him, and somehow he didn't belong in the caldron or icebox of whatever "feeling" state I was in. I've learned to begin not by trying to clear my mind of everything, but taking him where my mind is already fastened, where my feelings are real. I don't have the kind of discipline that can empty my mind and emotions, to prepare a spotlessly clean and acceptable place to meet him. Instead I bring God to it all. He is big enough for that. When I'm in the presence of an accepting friend I can begin where I am, or I get to it soon in a relaxed conversation. The same thing works for me with God. Of course to be consciously in his presence I have acknowledged him, and when I have told him my state of mind and we have explored all the pressing things together (when there are pressing things), calm begins to come. Then there is room for praise and thanks.

After years of instruction that I should begin with adoration, the opposite turned out to be my experience. Now, at the end of time spent with him, seeing old and new things in Scripture, knowing I have felt his presence, I am motivated to give praise and thanks that are genuinely from my heart. After I'd gotten in touch with my feelings about this, I suddenly realized a difference between honestly not wanting to be alone with God, and being tempted by Satan to some other activity, when I would otherwise be focusing on God.

The example of Jesus spending long times in prayer with his Father may spur us on to try for the same thing. Obviously this time was longed for by Jesus and was satisfying to him. 1 John 1:9 says that our confession of known sin will result in our being cleansed from all unrighteousness, so we can come before God in the same righteousness as Jesus. Perhaps the big difference is that Jesus knew his Father and the pleasure of being with him so well. He had no doubt about where his power and guidance came from. We are so slow to learn to know God. We so quickly feel self-reliant.

If we find personal devotions unrewarding, we'll never get to true meditation. Perhaps western culture itself has taken away the tools for meditation. Our materialism and affluence may discourage us from mulling over life in our inner recesses. If Christians meditate for long, we discover our feelings and have to come to terms with them. The feelings we aren't in touch with, or are ashamed to own, get in our way and we quit.

Trying to copy the experience of someone else can make us uncomfortable with God. The victories and satisfactions of others won't always fit the size and shape of my own need. Generally, "sharing" takes place only out of positive experiences. I am expected to reply affirmatively when someone says, "Isn't God good?" because what has happened was good from his or her point of view. I may not be having this feeling, even though I'm in intellectual agreement. God is *always* good and as we mature in him this fact will help us steadily build more positive feelings. But that must come from within. We must allow ourselves and others the personal momentary "feeling" experience. Guilt because we don't share someone's experience isn't helpful in being comfortable with God. Growth will help us enter more and more genuinely into the experiences of others.

Each Christian has an individual experience of God. God has a wonderful capacity for bringing me along my own path to maturity. God has a tender way of revealing more of his personality and plan for me when I'm ready. Sometimes his way is to keep me almost jealously in sight, to guard me from destruction. He brings me along at a different pace and along different paths than he brings you. I experience things about him that you may not have known for yourself, and I'm sure you've known him in ways that I haven't.

My growth is uneven. For instance, it has taken me a long time to learn that because of God the Son living in me, I can stand before God the Father and not be ashamed. On the other hand, as soon as I became a Christian, because of God the Holy Spirit, I knew I would never be lonely again. Since then, even before marriage, I have never experienced loneliness. Before I was a Christian, I often cried before I slept. I suppose it was some kind of universal loneliness that is part of not knowing God. Yet I know many Christians who experience empty, disconsolate feelings of being alone. Of course the *facts* are that because of Jesus I was always acceptable to the Father, and we are never alone. But our feelings can belie the facts. They don't line up with truth.

God wants them to, but simply to restate the facts doesn't get rid of negative feelings.

Some people are guided well by "putting out fleeces," but fleeces don't work for everybody. Giving God deadlines doesn't always produce results. I know people who get things from God by a sort of bargaining. I also know it can be anxiety-producing to try getting things from him in these ways by following their example.

I begin to feel edgy when I try to emulate some giant of faith in Scripture. "If Gideon could do it, I can do it. If God did it for Gideon, he will do it for me." I'm blessed by the wonderful account of God's assurance to Gideon. For me the lesson of Gideon is that God can strengthen and confirm and provide success when he has called someone to do a job. He may, however, actually intend sending someone on a risky mission without that kind of guarantee. In Gideon we see a man with courage to ask God to meet him at the point of his weakness, and God did it. So I know that God can meet me at the point of my weakness, but in his own way and time.

We don't feel good about God when we think he is overwhelmable, when we think we've handed him a hot potato he can't handle. I remember a friend who was worried that she had prayed either too hard or not hard enough for a man who lingered at death's door. Had her praying kept him from death and her lack of praying kept him from health? Gradually I've come to realize that God really is sovereign, and that's a good feeling.

We don't feel good about God when we've made him like ourselves—only a shade bigger and better, something like the gods of the Greeks and Romans, someone with whom we can play games. He isn't going to play games with us. He isn't going to shape us by clichés. "Let go and let God" is one cliché I tried on for a long time and found it didn't fit. He isn't going to pounce on us through someone's aggressive personality or guide us primarily from a book someone is enthusiastic about. He may not put us in the framework of the conference outline of one of his best-known speakers or hold us to the principles of a popular seminar leader. My fear of not conforming to some secure pattern is slowly leaving me. To be free from the need to conform, to be free from the need not to conform, is a pleasant feeling. God can use people who have the feel of freedom. It is freedom limited by the demands of love, but that is big freedom.

I'm not sure of the theological word for a certain quality of God that allows the feeling of freedom to deepen. We sense that quality as his ability to adjust us to our circumstances, our circumstances to us, and all of it to his will. His gift of responsible freedom allows us the privilege of making mistakes without fear. Our mistakes are covered by his flexibility.

Of course what I'm saying is "All things work together for good to those who love God." But when we think of what is involved in making this "work," it is an awesome quality of God. Not long ago I felt that a friend had made a major mistake. It had the earmarks of a brash and thoughtless act, and I regretted that it had happened. But in ensuing days, good things came of it. Looking back I realize that there was no way God would have let that become a disastrous thing, for my friend loves God with a whole heart. I think the only bad things that remain will be in the lives of those who somehow will miss God's point of view.

As God feeds the soil for our growth, he wants us to use our emotions to help evaluate our spiritual condition. When we sense something amiss in what has been handed to us from someone else, we can think through our uneasiness. We know that sickness and death carry strong negative feelings. Disappointments can feel terrible. It's wrong for us to try to override these legitimate experiences with a false cheer we foist on people because we can't handle our negative feelings. Persecution for righteousness' sake would feel bad. I imagine that Paul and Silas experienced a change from feelings of injustice and outrage to rejoicing in that Philippian jail. Perhaps their songs came at midnight because their negative feelings had to be thought through to the place where singing was possible (Acts 16:25).

The crucial thing in our relationship to God is to bring all our feelings into the light of his love, to work them through with him and with those he gives to help us in the body of Christ. God's best advertisers are those who have "tasted and eaten" from life's table. His best encouragers are those involved in a growing relationship with him, because they're in touch with themselves as well. They have used their feelings as tools to build this relationship.

Notes

1. C. S. Lewis, *The Problem of Pain* (New York: Macmillan, 1948) p. 29.

Feelings and the Bible 5

C. Peter Wagner, who is well informed about how God is working today in various cultures, recently said, "Ever since he created Adam, God has had one great project, to communicate to people." When God spoke, he did it in the framework of human capacity. He spoke through people to people, through people with feelings to people with feelings.

Feelings have a double role in relation to Scripture: how we feel about Scripture, and the part feelings play in it. A friend of mine responds intellectually when someone asks him how he feels about a book, but my own tendency would be to give my emotional reaction. Any book can receive either kind of appraisal, and the Bible justifiably elicits both kinds. No book has been more hotly debated, and hot debate is certainly a marriage of emotion and intellect. Our emotions are involved in how personally relevant the Bible becomes to us, and we haven't yet plumbed the depths of the emotions *in* it.

A friend and I once tried to describe the approach we'd learned at a school then unique in teaching an inductive method of Bible study[1]: how to arrive at biblical truths by studying all the particular parts. We decided to call it a "feel for the Scripture," by which we meant a confidence in approaching the Bible, born of study methods we'd learned.

Basic to a secure feeling about Scripture is the refreshing mental exercise of affirming its authority. The writers of the Westminster Confession long ago listed the sixty-six books of the Bible and then said, "... all of which are given by inspiration of God to be the rule of faith and life." The Lausanne Covenant, drawn up in Switzerland in 1974, says that the Bible "... is without error in all that it affirms."

When I became a Christian I accepted this on the word of older friends in Christ. Over the years I've had my own convictions about coming wholeheartedly to the same resting place. Scripture is central as long as it lives through the Persons of the Trinity. If all Scripture were destroyed, God would still be the same. While we struggle, understandably, over translations and methods of study and theories of inspiration, God wants us to see that the Bible exists to show us himself.

Another aspect of confidence about the Bible is a certain feeling of personal ownership. Of course it's the universal possession of all believers, and "no prophecy of Scripture is a matter of one's own interpretation" (2 Peter 1:20). But in another equally valid sense it is *my* book. The Holy Spirit is my teacher, so no other mediator between myself and the written pages of Scripture is necessary. I can read it eagerly, lightly, slowly, dully, with sharpened perception or "sightless" eyes. No formulas or approaches or conditions given by anyone should keep believers from feeling that it is their own, a treasured thing that we love and are at home with. Ownership of the Bible's contents shouldn't elude us. We shouldn't be anxious about whether we're using it in a way that will please anyone else—as if that person owned it more than we do.

We tend to enclose the Bible in a tightness that doesn't let us see it for all it is. Wilbur W. White, who founded the Biblical Seminary, said, "The message of any book of the Bible is greater than the sum of its parts." We miss the big messages of each book and the giant-sized proclamations of

Scripture when we fail to sense this principle.

A common, inadequate pattern is to try to find particular verses to back up great truths. It's the opposite of arriving at truth from our own study. Instead, we're trying to "prove" something we've been told. We feel unsure of a truth if we can't find a chapter and verse to substantiate it in so many words. One such truth is "God accepts me just the way I am." The verse, "While we were yet sinners, Christ died for us" (Romans 5:8), doesn't say exactly that. "Him who comes to me I will not cast out" (John 6:37) doesn't say that either. I can't find a verse that says it in these exact words, but the message gets through in the totality of Scripture.

A long time ago I knew that "Jesus loves me." Where do I find that in the Bible? I don't. "God is love" doesn't talk about *me*. Jesus doesn't ever say "you" meaning exactly "me." John 17:20 helps, but I find out that "Jesus loves me" from the Bible's total message.

Another truth is that all people are equal in God's sight. He doesn't like slavery, for example, or one person making another subservient in any way. "There is neither Jew nor Greek, there is neither slave nor free, there is neither male nor female" (Galatians 3:28). That comes close, but we can wriggle out of it. "He makes his sun rise on the evil and on the good, and sends rain on the just and on the unjust" (Matthew 5:45). That helps us, but it doesn't explicitly say it. "Man looks on the outward appearance, but the Lord looks on the heart" (1 Samuel 16:7) adds something but doesn't really clinch it. The truth comes through when our eyes and hearts are open to the total picture the Bible gives us.

We miss a healthy confidence in our approach to Scripture when we take verses out of their setting and isolate them. Sometimes this can be done without changing the meaning, but often it can't. Cults and sub-Christian religious groups can't thrive unless they do this. When the Bible is used as a hammer instead of a help, we get a bad feeling toward it; this often happens when a single verse or phrase is lifted out of context. The phrase "in Christ" communicates belonging, peace, rest. But those good feelings are mine in spite of a sermon I heard based on those words, which seemed to place me in a sterile box, "in Christ," where I should be feeling no puzzles, no problems, no mixed-up responses. I knew of no way to step out of these to get into this place "in Christ." Truth can be made to feel like a trap when verses aren't surrounded by the "before and after" things God has said.

The Bible was written without divisions into chapters and verses. It was divided into chapters in 1228 by a man named Stephen Langton and then into verses in 1551 by Robert Stephanus. The story goes that Stephanus did the verses while riding on horseback, and the horse must have stumbled a bit because they are sometimes split in very odd places![2] To restore the "feel" of the original, one effective Bible teacher uses a "manuscript" method and has whole books mimeographed without verses or chapters as they were first written.

Now, what about feelings in the Bible? Does the content of the Bible itself have anything to say about feelings? Chapter and verse? It's like asking, "Where do we find blood in the body?" Feelings saturate the entire Bible.

Clues to finding feelings in the Bible came to me from further principles of inductive study formulated by Dr. White. One is this: "Bring nothing to Scripture. Rather, take everything from it." Is this possible? We all have preconceived notions and ideas planted in us that we can't "forget." But it's more possible than you might think to leave behind old impressions and pretend that the Bible is brand-new each time you go to it. The Holy Spirit wants to help us in this process. The Bible never stops giving new insights from familiar passages. If we try to read it each time as though we've never seen it before, we find new truths. If you're growing in Christ, you aren't the same person from day to day, and the Bible has an astonishing way of being alive to where you are. Seeing new things gets us past the surface, and right underneath are the feelings of the people of Scripture who wrote it and the people about whom they wrote.

We think we know all the facts of a certain Bible account. When we read a particular narrative again, we tend to see only the things we saw before, which we bring back to it as we read. Or if we've been taught and have committed ourselves to a certain doctrine, perhaps a particular view of eschatology, we bring that view to Scripture and see only passages supporting it. How do we counteract that? One seminary professor threw away all her previous study notes before beginning a new course in a book of the Bible, and studied it again as though she'd never seen it before. She was legendary for the excitement of her classes.

Recently I had been reading through 1 Peter to grasp the whole letter. One morning as I began it again ("Peter, an apostle..."), a feeling of impatience gripped me. I thought, if every Bible writer had known that countless individuals for nearly 2,000 years would pore over every word they might have hesitated to pick up a pen, or whatever they wrote with, even under the guidance of the Spirit! Anyway, I was tired of the first two verses. But I stopped and asked the Holy Spirit to show me something new. Almost at once the name *Peter* stood out in bold letters. How would I have felt as a first-century Christian getting a letter from Peter? I thought how I'd feel if someone would write me a letter about C. S. Lewis and his work, someone who had lived three years with him. My excitement and gratitude would know hardly any bounds. But Peter had lived with the Lord himself, shoulder to shoulder with God, and perhaps had experienced deeper emotional involvement with him than any other disciple. He had thought through the implications of those years a thousand times. How worthwhile to spend time with what he wrote. I began again with renewed interest. The Bible is always worthy of attention because it is God's message to us, but the "bare bones" of that intellectual grasp need the "flesh of feeling."

Another helpful principle is this: "Study the Bible firsthand." This means knowing Bible truth for ourselves, and not merely from sermons, teaching, or even good books about it. Books and commentaries deal less with the emotionally laden words and phrases than with doctrines and facts. Studying firsthand with open minds brings us the feelings of Scripture.

A third principle in discovering feelings is: "Surround the facts with imagination as you study them." The people were real people, the situations alive. Let's try this with Mark 2:1-12.

Jesus is preaching in a small crowded house, packed with people who can't shower even once a week. We aren't sure of the weather outside, but it's hot in there. There is some quiet attentiveness, but restlessness too, here and there. Someone brushes away the flies that seem to be everywhere. Jesus is aware that among his listeners are some with critical spirits. Others don't care much about what he says but are looking for a miracle. This is an important time for Jesus, because he had told his disciples that he considered preaching a higher priority in his ministry than healing.

Then there's an interruption, a stirring near the door, and the muttering of protests. A group of people are pressing to get in. The noise dies down for a few minutes, and suddenly there is scraping overhead. The attention of the audience shifts to the ceiling. Dust and splinters of tile splatter down on Jesus and those around him. What he is saying is important. There is tenseness as he absorbs criticism from religious leaders, but now comes this inescapable interruption.

Whose nervous system was ever more sensitive than his? He feels compassion for people, pain when others are in pain. He allows his most important activity to be set aside for a healing as the paralytic is lowered in front of him. In perfect integration of purpose and feeling, the healing time leads into a teaching session: a demonstration of whole love, an example of emotional maturity. We're impressed with the magnificence of the One we follow. To me as a mother, often pressed and not always in control, Jesus shines in a situation like that.

Feelings help us grasp the doctrines of Scripture. We experience the aversion, confusion, ache, and ambivalence surrounding "sin" and "conviction" and "repentance"; the warmth and comfort of "mercy" and "grace," and "forgiveness."

Let the Apostle Paul's emotions aid us in learning from him. Consider Romans 9:1, 2. His anguish, sorrow, and self-sacrifice over his lost Jewish brothers could stir us to caring and witness. In 2 Corinthians 5:2, 4, he wrote about groaning and sighing with anxiety while in our earthly bodies. How he identified with life's pain! What does that say to us in our complacency as we turn away from indescribable suffering in large areas of our world? In 2 Corinthians 11:28, Paul spoke of the daily pressure of his concern for the welfare of all the churches, his identification with weak believers, his indignation when someone was caused to fall. How often sorrow permeated his letters as he agonized over the rebukes he knew he had to make. Feel with him. Aren't we the keepers of our brothers and sisters in Christ? When we are provoked to rebuke someone, do sorrow and sadness precede it? Examples like this abound, but we seldom consider the emotional openness with which Paul expressed his relationships with people. We talk about being vulnerable—he is an example. Apart from the great importance of his doctrinal contributions, I love Paul for both his commitment and his humanity.

It's true that the emotions in the Bible came out of a culture different from our own. There, feelings flowed; here, ours most often don't—until they're out of control. Of course those people didn't handle all feelings well, but perhaps they were in better emotional health than we are with our buryings and smotherings. The expressed anger of Esau was used to bring Jacob to the repentance he needed as the leader named "Israel." What if Esau had stuffed his hate under his shirt and tie and pretended everything was OK? To slice off the obvious emotions of Scripture as inapplicable to us is less damaging than disposing of the miracles, perhaps, but it has the flavor of "surgical heresy." Let's hasten to get biblical about feelings.

Few people are comfortable with the book of Revelation, yet most of us are curious about what it means. It's a beautiful book to read for feelings. We can be so concerned about its interpretation that we miss what God is saying plainly. The plain and the difficult are both packed with emotion. Read it from start to finish, just you and the Holy Spirit and maybe a few friends, expecting to find and feel great things. You will find your own special places in it. Chapter 5 always stirs me, but from beginning to end the book "feels." It is a revelation to see how much is understandable, and more so as present history develops. Dr. Ted Engstrom, without coming to settled conclusions, challenges us that the black horse of the apocalypse may be loose today as we wake up to the fact of widespread famine.[3]

The Old Testament is rich with feeling. It's probably unnecessary to mention the Psalms, with everything from praise to imprecation: joy and hate, gladness and pain, assurance and doubt, comfort and sorrow, trust and suspicion, forgiveness and revenge. I'm sure one reason we cherish the Psalms is that they're so emotion-laden; they always speak to our hearts. How on earth have we ever studied them and forgotten how to look inside ourselves as those writers did?

Are any passages more pathetic and heart-wrenching than Isaiah 5:1-7 and Isaiah 53? The book of Esther and the story of the Shunammite woman in 2 Kings 4:8-37 are examples of deep feelings under control. Even Numbers and Leviticus are full of feelings just beneath the surface. Feel with those involved in the sacrificial system. How long has it been since you felt the pain in the Lamentations or enjoyed the sexual delight of the Song of Solomon? The book of Ruth is a good example of the fact that a lot of loving goes on in the Bible even when the word *love* doesn't appear. Look for it.

As I sit here thinking about the Bible, it seems almost wrong to describe one passage as more emotion-filled than another. To do a thorough job I should quote Genesis through the Revelation, rather than cite some passages at random. You can quickly make your own list.

Why do we have favorite passages? Because in addition to the truths they've given us, we're emotionally attached to them. They have spoken to something inside us and we feel it. If Scripture has become dull, there may be many reasons. One could be that we haven't yet learned to look there for feelings.

Notes

1. The Biblical Seminary in New York, since become The New York Theological Seminary and no longer chiefly a center for inductive Bible study.

2. Howard Tillman Kuist, *These Words Upon Thy Heart* (Richmond, Va., John Knox Press, 1947) pp. 100, 101.

3. Ted W. Engstrom, "Lo, The Black Horse Cometh!", *World Vision* February, 1975.

Feelings and the Bad Old Days

6

Looking back into history and watching the church live through the ages shows us that Christians have initiated most of the world's educating and healing ministries right up to our own era. It also helps us realize that while our weaknesses and failures aren't new, they are ever with us. It's hard for many people now to look back with nostalgia on recent decades. There have been so many "bad old days" that they associate with Christianity.

Painful memories in my own life include visits to my Christian grandparents. My grandfather tried to make me promise to wear my skirts longer (in the late thirties), not to wear lipstick, or date until I was twenty-five. The bad old days were junior and senior high school years when I spent Monday through Saturday thinking of ways to get out of going to church on Sunday. I always ended up stiffnecked and stiffbacked in the pew, waiting for the inevitable lengthy and emotion-packed "invitation." With God I would have no roller-skating (because they played dance music at the rink), no makeup or jewelry or curls. Christians wore drab clothes. I swore to myself I would die before giving in to God under those circumstances.

The bad old days for me included going to church summer camp where the daytime, however happy, was dimmed by dread of the evening meetings. I always sat in the back row, but counselors formed a rear guard to block escape. Once at the close of an evening, as I was bent over to avoid questions, I was grateful to a woman who mistakenly said, "You'd better leave her alone. She's under conviction." The interrogators left.

Although Sunday church-going was a painful and inexorable duty, my parents, watchful and tender and caring about life in general, left me alone about God the rest of the week. The church we attended happened to be the one closest to our house, and we belonged in some church on a Sunday. I learned a lot of hymns in those years and made one lasting friend, but paid a high price. When I found myself at college I was confirmed in the Episcopal church, the quietest, least legalistic atmosphere I could find, where they instructed me and let me take it from there. I believed all the facts about Jesus, whom I finally met personally at the First Presbyterian Church in Berkeley four years later.

There are many whose early experiences were far more miserable than my own, like my friend who was made to kneel at her mother's coffin to confess her sins. There were miserable days in the childhood of A. S. Neill, the educator who founded a school in England called Summerhill. His book by that name is a marvel of misunderstanding about the Christian faith and authority. He puts down both at every opportunity, simultaneously showing a love and sensitivity for children. Neill tells how, caught at six years of age in sex play with his little sister, they were "severely thrashed; and I was locked in a dark room for hours, and then made to kneel down to ask forgiveness from God."[1] His later conclusions: "Both the Jewish and Christian religions hate the flesh,"[2] and "The religious hate of the vile flesh makes corporal punishment popular in religious regions."[3] Thousands have flocked to Neill's position, and the church has received a good deal of scorn. Perhaps A. S.

Neill never knew the truth, that Jesus did not condemn the love we all have for our flesh.

Others have had experiences that were less stringent and in some ways the opposite of those painful ones. For them there were no unreasonable emotional demands but, instead, severe pressure to conform to authoritative unbiblical standards: the "no cards, no movies" syndrome. As an adult I have heard many uncomfortable discussions over whether young people should dance. How feelings flew, giving me a sinking sense of "majoring in minors." The issue of whether or not to dance was more important in those heated conversations than the cross, the hugeness of God, and his ability to take care of things.

A distraught mother called the afternoon before a school prom. By that time her daughter had talked her into buying a formal and at the eleventh hour the mother's scruples against dancing had risen to screaming proportions. Should she let her daughter go? Neither Yes nor a No at that point would have solved the problem in their home.

The bad old days of a recent, fast-fading era were characterized by discouraging any show of emotion, except for a smile in the presence of other Christians, whether or not your heart was breaking. Disapproval about expressing feeling was accompanied by close attention to doctrinal purity. Negative feelings were closeted.

Also characteristic of past years was the carefully sheltered Christian nest. Then in the teen years the nestlings began to realize there was an exciting world from which they had been largely secluded. As they became adults they had to carry Christian faith into the unknown. Some have done this successfully, finding God big enough to handle any challenge. For others the world's rewards have been more meaningful than their cushioned faith. Today the world impinges so heavily on everyone that a sheltered nest is almost an impossibility.

A significant bad thing in the church is pressure upon

children to be perfect. An awful tension surrounds the tendency to base parental approval on performance. I know many instances where this pride, this desire to produce children who conform to everything within the framework of a particular local church or denomination, has stifled spontaneity and eventually turned children away. The church has often encouraged children to become people-pleasers, a role that the earliest Christians rightly rejected.

Some sins are more insidious than outright legalism or doctrinal coldness or unrealistic demands upon children to conform and perform. These are the sins accompanying affluence and the marriage of Christianity to non-Christian values in our materialistic culture. Dr. David Hubbard once said that children from Christian families often accept the values they learn at home and church in one tight package—the death and resurrection of Jesus, the need for personal salvation, loyalty to the local church program, "keeping up with the Joneses," racial prejudice, commitment to the status quo. When they become more thoughtful, they may toss out the whole package. Sometimes young people untie the package and examine the contents. Blessed are those who have quiet support in the sifting process. The "Jesus generation" has questioned many false values in our society. Generally, though, Christians seem slow to divorce themselves from unholy marriage to a materialistic culture.

Two facts prompt me to wade through a little of the unpleasantness of the bad years. One is that these unbiblical patterns touched the lives of so many Americans and furnished them with reasons to keep away from churches. The second is that those days sowed the seeds of bad feelings about God and his people that have taken root and grown in thousands of Christian lives. We can't ignore the terrible false guilts behind these bad feelings.

Thousands tuned God out and have never tuned him back in. A psychotherapist recently said that many of her clients who are out of touch with the church had significant Christian training in their earlier years. The church of my own early experience had a lengthy roster of dropouts.

Thousands of others who left the channels open and kept on believing have turned the volume low and remained somewhat guarded members of evangelical congregations. They are often more knowledgeable about doctrines and the Bible than many new Christians who are free in spirit to forge ahead. In their thirties, forties, fifties, sixties, and seventies, they are among the Lord's most faithful and trustworthy stewards. They give time, money, and energy, but the pain isn't gone. In spite of discomfort, they stay in the church because they know that Jesus is the One to follow; they are "in his bonds." As I have thought about this, the old hymn came to mind:

> Other refuge have I none,
> Hangs my helpless soul on Thee.
> Leave, oh, leave me not alone;
> Still support and comfort me.

People who have remained loyal to Jesus Christ in spite of years of legalism or cold doctrine or false values are sometimes accused of being ashamed of the gospel because they find it difficult to witness freely. They are suspect for being unable to verbalize their faith readily before others, and for their reluctance to break the mold of caution in this respect. They aren't ashamed of the real gospel. Perhaps some unconscious resistance remains in them from days when inviting people to church wasn't easy, since it wasn't the most attractive fellowship with its rules and regulations. Perhaps it's impossible for them to express the good news of Jesus effectively without open gladness, and open gladness calls for expressing feelings long discouraged. Perhaps they have buried feelings of shame for the context in which the gospel was often presented: unloving, impersonal, buttonholing, "gospel blimp" techniques.

The Bad Old Days

A gracious and dedicated woman who has long been committed to many causes in the evangelical church unwittingly voiced this one day. She said that in spite of her genuine love for the Lord it had always been difficult for her to speak openly about him. But she had recently brought herself to the place where she could invite neighbors to a Bible study in her home. How often we hear people say, "I'm not the type who can speak about my faith. I can only live it." Although Peter suggests that a holy life goes a long way as a witness, you can't communicate the cross by living it—and very few of us live that impressively, even if we *could* speak the cross by our works. The gospel does need words. But my heart feels the hurt of failure to combine belief with its articulate expression. Feelings about this have been put away, ignored, starved.

The matter of false guilt is important in this reflection. I have lived with false guilt. It is a ghastly, life-sapping, depression-producing thing. It is a *feeling* tied up with an *attitude* toward oneself. It is different from true guilt, which also feels bad but comes because we have sinned, and in God's eyes a wrong must be made right. False guilt is only a feeling. There has been no sin; it is an emotional response to something we have supposed is sin.

Although the whole subject of guilt is very complex, Paul Tournier helps us with the difference between true and false guilt. He says, "God's thoughts and men's thoughts; judgments of God and judgments of men; that is a clear formulation between true guilt and false guilt."[4] Responding to the ideas of human beings rather than the thoughts of God, people feel they've sinned when they really haven't. For instance, the blanket prohibition against movies produced false guilt in the person who went to one, because that idea was from the thoughts of men, not of God, and produced the judgments of men, not of God. Real guilt is like being in jail until God unlocks the door. False guilt is like being in jail until we realize that we've shut the door ourselves and no one ever locked it.

The judgments of men are so easily arrived at and so easily enforced upon other believers because the consciences of Christians are sensitive. The majority of Christians want to be good and to keep the rules. To be a sower of false guilt is a heinous sin, which God will judge in the way he judged the Pharisees: "You load men with burdens hard to bear, and you yourselves do not touch the burdens with one of your fingers" (Luke 11:46).

It pays to know God's thoughts and to know them well. When we know the "whole counsel of God" from Scripture, we can be careful not to live with human judgments and force them on others. The whole counsel of God includes Romans 14 which instructs us in the delicate matter of not doing anything to offend a weaker brother, even if the act in itself isn't a matter of sin. But as Paul Morris points out, it's new Christians toward whom we must be sensitive in this, not the old "salts" who have been in the church for years.[5]

There is a dignity in coming to God with sin and guilt and receiving his gracious and unconditional pardon. In our congregation, Dr. Raymond Ortlund often encourages us to "keep short accounts with God." After confession and forgiveness, all remaining feelings of guilt are false. False guilt is not erased by confession. But when real sin is forgiven, there need not be any false guilt. Witness the joy of David when he confessed his sin.

It's helpful to associate the forgiveness of real guilt with justification (our being "right" with God), and the release from false guilt with sanctification (our growth or identification with God). Feelings of false guilt stand in the way of growth. Satan is the only one who profits. False guilt suits his purposes. As far as he's concerned, a burdened believer is as good as a drunk in the gutter—perhaps better, because the drunk isn't representing a joy-giving God.

We can become free from false guilts as we recognize them for what they are, as we comprehend more fully the scope of our acceptance. After real sin is confessed and justification is ours, false guilt may remain, for three reasons. First, we may not believe that God has really forgiven us. The only antidote for this is to know God better, and the only way to do that is to meet him in the Scripture. Does he keep his promises there? Yes, he does. Is Jesus the kind of person who is trustworthy? Yes, he is. Will he keep his promise to forgive us and to enfold us? Yes, he will.

A second reason for false guilt may be that our conscience hasn't been well taught. Perhaps we must unlearn some things that bother us but don't bother God, things that are "sin" to us and not to him. Again, the answer lies in learning what he tells us is sin in Scripture. The Bible is our filter.

A third reason may be that we haven't forgiven ourselves. The key here is to get rid of the attitude that we are our own prosecutor, judge, and jailer. We must learn to accept what is going on inside, to stop our self-flagellation, to become judgment-free. Paul said, "With me it is a very small thing that I should be judged by you or any human court. I do not even judge myself" (1 Corinthians 4:3).

Habits are often difficult to change. Our efforts to become free of settled false guilt may be slow, but freedom is worth working toward. It is crucial to peace with God. Because true and false guilts "feel" alike, they get confused over the years when they aren't handled well. When false guilt isn't relieved by confession, it discourages more confessing. The bad feelings are woven into a tangled scrabble. So much junk is left over from years of unsuccessful efforts to live above guilt that many have stopped trying to sort it out.

Someone might say, "Let's forget all these bad old days and move on." The fact is you can't forget what has never been resolved. Paul says, "Forgetting what lies behind and straining forward to what lies ahead, I press on" (Philippians 3:13, 14). But in the next verse he qualifies this forward call by saying, "Let those of us who are mature be thus minded; and if in anything you are otherwise minded, God will reveal that also to you." Paul has left room for working through and resolving our bad feelings about the past, a discarding process that has to take place before we can be spiritually adult.

For years after I became a Christian, an altar call or even the most soft-sell invitation to Christ flooded me with involuntary emotional identification with anyone who might be struggling the way I did with the agony of indecision. What's involved in such a situation isn't our reason but our feelings. Even though reason told me that a particular invitation was a gentle, courteous one, without the old heavy-handed pressure, I would be uncomfortable. Now I can hear an invitation and pray rather than squirm, having worked through some bad old feelings.

Times have changed, but many conflicts with feelings remain. How do we get the bad old days to pass? First, we must want to get past them, to be willing to let them go. It's essential to be honest and not use them as excuses or rationalizations for not moving ahead where we feel blocked. During his forty years as a shepherd in Midian, Moses must have spent long hours with painful feelings left from the traumatic adventure that drove him from Pharaoh's court. Three verses in Exodus cover the incident, which must have had nationwide Egyptian news coverage. His loyalty and zeal toward his oppressed kinspeople had driven Moses to murder. He had offered himself as a deliverer, was rejected by his people, and was driven into exile. In Midian, his first reply to God's call was, "How will they know that *you* have sent me this time?" Is this a clue to how he still felt about his bad experience? But he remained open and honest as he talked to God. I think Aaron was willing to be included in God's plan because Moses had thoroughly shared his feelings with his brother. Aaron knew all about those bad old days.

The Bad Old Days
69

It's essential in moving away from the past to open our-selves to God and to another person, to allow the anger or resentment or reproach or sadness or confusion to be un-covered, expressed—confessed, if need be—and then drained away. We can seek the help of understanding pas-tors and qualified counselors to unhook us from the things we're hung up on—the hooks that are fastened firmly by our feelings. For those who've left the church and are gone, we can only pray and trust in the perfect justice of God. Perhaps in our hope for widespread renewal, these people may be reached again. I urge those who know about these old days only by hearsay not to be impatient or to judge. There has been too much of that. Only those who have stuck with the faith through it all know the painful duality of being part of the body of Christ but not feeling joyful in it.

If we aren't conscious of our feelings, the bad old days will always be around in new disguises. When people be-come Christians, they're thrust into the Christian commu-nity from a culture where the values are almost never the values of God. The movement from one commitment to another, to be lasting and fruit-producing in new Christians, must be accompanied by an atmosphere where conflicting feelings can be worked through. Otherwise, when the first joy of conversion fades, when God seems to withdraw the excitement and replace it with the challenge, trouble can come.

Those who have studied church growth tell us that the first few weeks in the new life of the believer are the most crucial. As we glibly tell new Christians not to trust feelings but to rely on facts, we fail to help them use their feelings well. Doubts and questions arise from the equally glib as-surances we give. "If any man is in Christ, he is a new creature; the old things passed away, behold, new things have come" (2 Corinthians 5:17 NASB). The context of that verse is Paul's resolution of the conflict with the tensions of the flesh and our ultimate complete transformation. This verse refers to our position in Christ. It refers to ourselves as the heroes and heroines whose victory is already written at the end of the story, although we're still in the middle of our mightiest battles. But we often use this verse, particularly from the King James Version, to assure new Christians that "all things have become new." New things have come, but *all* is not new. There is that huge subconscious part of our minds still unclaimed for God in the present, but of course included in the final victory. Conquering that territory of the subconscious is part of what growth means.

It's often out of the subconscious mind that conflicts and subsequent bad feelings begin to come. Some people, who have reasonably good emotional health when they come to Christ, grow quickly and stay steady. Those with big psychological difficulties will probably meet those difficulties again as Christians. Sam Shoemaker explained why we may not see immediate answers to our prayers for someone's growth or salvation, even though our requests are close to the heart of God. The Holy Spirit may be working deep in the person's mind, getting their subconscious mind ready to meet the change when their conscious mind accepts Christ or makes a forward decision. Without digging deeper into this complex subject, it's important to understand that new Christians must have an accepting atmosphere (that is, one devoid of conditional approval based on performance), in which to sort out their confusing feelings.

There are bad days ahead for the new believer who finds his or her new walk not up to par with the rest of the believing community and then senses their disapproval. What is the source of disillusionment? An old temptation that still kicks up? Temptation doesn't mean that salvation is gone but rather that the opportunity for growth has come. Is the old environment still around? Then extra support and encouragement are called for. Whatever the problem, if the only "help" given is to be told to cling to the facts, to forget feelings, the new Christian will either fall away or fall into new problems. Then one more person will have "bad old days" in his memory bank.

Notes

1. A. S. Neill, *Summerhill: A Radical Approach to Child Rearing* (New York: Hart Publishing Co., 1960), p. 207.

2. *Ibid.*, p. 373.

3. *Ibid.*, p. 359.

4. Paul Tournier, *Guilt and Grace* (New York: Harper & Row, 1962), p. 71.

5. Paul Morris, *Love Therapy* (Wheaton, Illinois: Tyndale House Publishers, 1974), p. 108.

Feelings in the Church

My life is bound up with the people who are Lake Avenue Congregational Church in Pasadena, California. Through that fellowship I see people becoming Christians. I see people making changes in their lives. I see people supporting each other in many ways. I see some people opening themselves so we can know each other deeply and honestly. A lot of loving goes on. I see people giving their lives in service in the community, around the United States, and quietly going off to Chad, Kenya, Ivory Coast, Ghana, France, Belgium, Panama, Brazil, Colombia, Japan, Taiwan, etc., in our large overseas missionary force. Unfortunately, my description of the "body of Christ gathered" does not fit many congregations in our land.

The working philosophy of our congregation is summed up in a book by our pastor, Dr. Raymond C. Ortlund, *Lord, Make My Life a Miracle*. We seek to build the life of the church around three priorities. First, there must be fresh and renewed commitment to God through Jesus Christ. Second, we must have warm commitment to the body of believers at home and abroad. Third, we seek to commit ourselves to the work in the world God calls us to do. The world doesn't need placid churches. If the life of God is in any congregation, "the world, the flesh, and the devil" will be there too, and our problems will be common ones. As our pastor says, dead churches have no problems and they cost nothing, personally or financially. But wherever the action is, feelings will be in evidence.

Twice in the past two years our congregation shared an experience we called "waiting on God." Each time it was a series of evenings when six or seven hundred people met to spend extra time with him. Feelings and action were always in beautiful balance. As we expected, we were all led by God into sharing, singing, quietness. I myself "turned a corner" because there was lots of quiet time to look inward. The atmosphere was free of judgment or emphasis on performance. At such a time the weak and the strong are equal, and it felt good to be together with that kind of acceptance.

Christians don't consistently meet each other with this Spirit-guided respect. If I always view every believer as an honored child of God, for whose life God alone is ultimately responsible, my whole feeling for that person is accepting and right. Acceptance has the feeling of relief, security, hopefulness. I approach every person as accountable only to God, created by him, born again only by his will. That individual is special.

One purpose of being the body of Christ is to develop the uniqueness of each member, to allow every person to become what God has made him or her to be. Often in this effort "no support comes from the churches, for the churches have forgotten that the concerns of Christianity are for the individual and we are preoccupied with numbers."[1] Feelings are strategic in the process of allowing each person to grow, and handling feelings well is indispensable to the health of the whole body of Christ.

Impatience with feelings is sometimes heightened when Christians are gathered, as though emotions are enemies of sound doctrine or a hindrance to sturdy and steady growth. If we stop to fiddle with feelings, things won't get done. Yet the oneness Paul stresses in Philippians 1:27—2:2 won't develop when our feelings about togetherness are elusive and confused.

It is, of course, the leaders who strike the notes that let us know whether we can allow our feelings to aid us in growth, whether we can be ourselves, or whether we must play a role in which we can be sure of acceptance, performing so that we get a "well done" from them. Accept leadership with fear and trembling!

Leadership invites insecurity: you must be better to lead, all eyes are on your performance, other leaders must be pleased. A leader may feel unsure or nervous, but simply because of being a leader these feelings are unacceptable. Insecurity drives some leaders to judgment and criticism. A psychological principle as old as history is that one stays on top by finding flaws in others. People who can most readily verbalize and command attention are most often lifted to leadership, and though these qualities are possibly necessary, they have their attendant fault: the temptation to keep strong by seeing the weakness of others.

It's possible to be a strong leader and still be feeling-oriented. Through lack of awareness about feelings, many leaders defeat themselves. Leadership calls for decisive action, not introspective meandering. So, serious and thoughtful leaders can come to the place where they aren't in touch with what is going on inside themselves. Emotions can unconsciously become masters. Decisions coming out of malaise can lack the wisdom characteristic of good leadership, because clear thinking has been hampered by uncared-for feelings.

Badly handled feelings affect both leaders and followers in the church. The worst offender is the spirit of nonacceptance and judgment. A second is the failure to face what is emotionally real in our striving for spiritual integration. A third is the neglect of feelings in learning to love one another. A fourth is our lack of understanding of how feelings of love are significant in obedience. A fifth is the twisting of feelings when we face the difficult matter of "discipline" in the church. After considering these, we may see other areas where we violate handling feelings with integrity.

(1) Jesus condemned judging, and so can we. "Judge not, that you be not judged" (Matthew 7:1). A spirit of judgment can creep insidiously into the corporate life of the church, even in the face of an overt effort to promote love. When we don't accept people, it's because we're evaluating them. Evaluating is a subtle form of judgment and leads to trouble. If I'm not accepted for myself, if my "feeling" antennae pick up vibes that I am found wanting for *any* reason, I'm baffled, disappointed, worried, frustrated, angry.

On the other hand, if *I* don't accept others exactly where they are, with what they have or don't have, I find myself envious, suspicious, indignant, defensive. All these negative feelings are buried because to acknowledge them might make me more unacceptable or uncomfortable than ever.

The spirit of judgment is fostered by thinking that what God is leading me to be (perhaps what someone else has told me to be or do) is what you also should become. That may make you feel that you and the Holy Spirit are inadequate together for guidance. Anyone can join in the game of "playing God." If you find yourself solving the problems of others, it may mean that you have a set of your own that you aren't able to solve. It's easier and less painful to tackle others' difficulties.

A spirit of judgment is sometimes seen in relationships based on the word *disciple* used as a verb. To "disciple" someone means to bring a less experienced Christian along the path to maturity. But the "discipled" person, if always on the receiving end, begins feeling a lack of worth, an inadequacy, which leads to defensiveness. In the body of Christ, only two-way relationships can grow. One couple decided after being "discipled" for awhile that it wouldn't work. They were expected to share their problems, to be accountable for certain growth and accomplishments, but if the discipling couple had their own goals and problems, they weren't shared. Prayer became one-way, too. The discipled couple had something to give, but felt put down without an opportunity to make a contribution. What could have been a mutually rewarding relationship had been sacrificed.

Judgment by others is often felt by those who don't participate in some program set up in the church. Such judgment leads to further nonparticipation. We may think we know what is best for everyone but in reality be blind and deaf to real needs, to the unmet longings of our friends in Christ. "As members of the Church we need to resist the temptation to give answers to questions that no one has asked, and deal with that in ourselves which prevents us from creating an atmosphere in which we and others can question."[2] Jesus was qualified to answer questions no one had asked, because he knew what was in people's minds. But if we do the deciding for others, we are denying that they are individuals with individual gifts and goals.

Because small groups are strategic instruments for building us up according to God's plan, they seem to be a special object of Satan's attack. He knows how to use a judgmental spirit. Effective small groups give us an opportunity to air the negatives in our lives in a comfortable setting. It's a little hard to grab someone by the elbow on a Sunday morning when everyone is hurrying to the sanctuary or home to dinner and say, "Look, Jane, I feel awful about something." The timing is obviously bad. But how good it is to rest inwardly in the presence of people who love each other just as they are.

I have witnessed the destruction of two small groups. Both succumbed to judgments that resulted from high expectations. Both failed to make the participants humanly comfortable with all the feelings connected with the challenge of daily living.

A friend once shared the hurt of feeling rejected by the

small group to which she and her husband had committed themselves. In the group she had asked, "What do you think it really means to 'walk by faith'?" Someone laughed and said, "You've been a Christian forever and you don't know that?" Someone added, "Stick around and you'll find out." It sounds barbaric, but it happened. Soon she and her husband felt that the time they spent in the group wasn't profitable and they "uncommitted" themselves. You may say, "That was pretty shallow commitment," or "Obviously, she should have told them how much she'd been hurt." Or you may find yourself judging the behavior of those who made such comments. How very easily we lead with our judgments rather than our love. Few of us have learned to handle hurts in mature enough ways to live comfortably with nonacceptance. Not much is productive in an uncomfortable small group.

My husband and I have had a very positive experience with a few friends. For example, we were once discussing 1 John 4:18, "Perfect love casts out fear." What could be simpler? But someone said, "I wonder what kind of fear that means." We began to understand in the context of the verse that it is fear of God's judgment, not necessarily fears arising from other sources. The "perfect love" is God's, not something we must attain. That adds a great deal of meaning to the verse and takes the pressure off it. In this small group we are free to be ourselves. There is laughter, unwinding, release, learning. It feels very good.

(2) Another violation of feelings arises from our tendency to "spiritualize" life. We try to reduce reality to a phony spiritual dimension. We fail to deal separately with what is emotional and what is spiritual (in the narrow sense) in our lives, often denying our humanity and the feelings that go with it. Two women came out of a planning meeting and spoke simultaneously. One said, "Now we'll see what the Lord will do." The other said, "Well, let's see what happens next." Both are dedicated and spiritually alert, but the

first one sounded more so. Sometimes, as in this case, it is spontaneous and genuine. When we are expecting God to do something, it's natural to say so. But it's easy to represent ourselves as more spiritual by the way we say things. It seems more spiritual to say, "God healed me" than it is to say, "I got well," although God is always in the healing.

We "spiritualize" illness and death by not allowing people to show sorrow. How unlike Jesus, a man of sorrows and acquainted with grief. Someone I know felt great sorrow over a dying friend and cried about it on more than one occasion. Something in her feels very sensitive about illness that leads to death. A friend said, "You shouldn't cry. She's in God's hands and you have to leave her there." But Jesus wept. Though we may not fully understand why, we don't sense that it was an unnecessary or unspiritual act on his part. God gave us tears.

One young man was encouraged to rejoice over a serious, still undiagnosed illness of his wife, because it gave God an opportunity to do some great thing. I know a person who is afraid it's "unspiritual" to be sick. But listen to Paul's honest feelings as he speaks about the illness of Epaphroditus: "Indeed he was ill, near to death. But God had mercy on him, and not only on him but on me also, lest I should have sorrow upon sorrow. I am the more eager to send him, therefore, that you may rejoice at seeing him again and that I may be less anxious" (Philippians 2:27, 28). Paul was human and willing to say so.

Sometimes we assure the loved ones of even terminally ill people that healing *is* possible, with a certainty that implies not only probability but inevitability. Of course God can heal, but who compiles statistics on the disillusioned who were literally promised the earthly healing of a loved one who simply went on to be with God? There's more integrity when a follower of Mary Baker Eddy uses the word *healed* at a Christian Science funeral. If we can't admit human frailty of all kinds, then we blindly put on God a responsibility to keep promises that he hasn't made. Firm assurances of healing that prove to be dust and ashes arouse feelings of guilt in those who have instilled the false hope. Strained feelings invariably creep into the relationships of all involved.

Our failure to relate realistically to the big and little troubles of others often coincides with our inability to be in touch with our own negative feelings about trouble. We don't like to feel disconsolate, forlorn, frightened, dismayed, hopeless, weak, unhappy. We feel inadequate or shy with those who may be experiencing these emotions. Simplistic answers are easier than coping with negative feelings.

(3) We also violate feelings by leaving them out of loving. Working out relationships in love is a challenge that calls for opening ourselves to others. We can encounter misunderstanding and make mistakes. When we're accepted, or misunderstood, we *feel* it. Loving and feeling are inseparable. We fail to love well when we don't take feelings into account.

One way to tamper with the feelings of love is to use the phrase, "I love you," carelessly. We heed Jesus' command in John 13:34 and tend to say, "I love you," easily. But saying it can be a superficial, sinful thing unless it's said with integrity, backed by positive feelings and consistent acts. A reserved man I know is still getting over the experience of having someone put his arm around him saying, "I love you, brother," and then shortly afterward offend him in a shady business deal. We will continue to handle the expression of love shabbily when we do it to gain approval. Satan works for every meaningless "I love you" he can get.

An often repeated precept about love is: "You may not be able to love someone, but Jesus in you can love that person." How can I honestly divide God and "me" when it comes to loving? I'm not an empty pipe through which God pours pure love. God in me is teaching me to love, but a fragmentation claiming that God is using my body and voice and mind to love people like a dummy on a ventriloquist's lap is invalid. Perhaps I should say, "At least it doesn't work for me," but the truth is it doesn't work for anybody. It's painful for the honest person who tries it and knows it's phony, and it also comes through that way to the other person. Of course, we can act thoughtfully regardless of how we feel toward someone, but let's not call it love.

(4) An interesting connection exists between the feelings of love and obedience. Rachel Mitchell, a woman whose outer life of good acts is matched with a warm heart, asked a group of us, "How do you get more love?" Her answer, after our canned ones, was "Through obedience." What does obedience have to do with loving? When we obey God, we follow his direction into the needs of someone else, into the thick of life, into the arena of witnessing. We have to become loving—because obedience without the positive feelings of love is too painful. Jesus obeyed out of love. Consistent, extended obedience will never happen unless we're lovers.

In the presence of obedience, if we're honest we will recognize heavy negative feelings. We're asked by Scripture or by a prompting from the Holy Spirit or by someone to do something. Our feelings about it could be reluctance, annoyance, helplessness, aversion. We hear a command, and negative feelings cause us to pull back. Obedience often takes us into untried territory where we're uncomfortable. Or obedience takes us into old territory where we feel bored and discontented. Often we just stop obeying because we haven't admitted those negative feelings. But we can "hear" these feelings, admit them, and tell God that we know they're there, really part of us. How can we get them to God if we ignore them? When we've recognized what they are, we can make a clear decision: to obey or to disobey. Unhandled negative feelings cause us to bypass the command, often with excuses, sometimes in carelessness.

Feelings are adaptable; they aren't our enemies. When we have honestly recognized them and then obeyed, our feelings often fall into line and grow positive. It's then we have the sense that God is loving through us, because by ourselves we would have experienced only the negatives. His love in us triggers consistent good deeds and warm emotions: interest, optimism, anticipation, concern, determination.

(5) We often deal badly with feelings when we exercise "tough love" in the church. Love sometimes "drags us into court." Sometimes we think that a person must be removed from a church job, from the Sunday school, choir, or some other position. We can go at a delicate matter like this with hurtful tactics: a curt letter, a too-brief confrontation. Sometimes we must intrude in the life of a person who we know totters on shaky moral ground, who has committed an open and flagrant sin such as continued damaging gossip or adultery or lies or dishonesty in business.

"Tough love" must be exercised with a lot of care. Truth can paralyze and confuse. This is because our feelings are all mixed up. We aren't in touch with what's going on inside ourselves, the embarrassment, tension, nervousness, anger. We don't like the situation or what we have to say, and we turn our feelings to the person receiving the discipline. Our inner turbulence keeps us from meaningful touch with the one who is feeling attacked. Genuine sorrow is gentle and can come through when feelings are sorted out.

We sabotage our corporate health by mishandling feelings. For instance, we praise the person who announces that he has overcome his feelings and is "moving" in spite of them. But that won't last long unless overcoming has meant taking care of them.

One night a girl described how she'd come home from a retreat feeling pretty low. (This may happen more often than we realize, because we generally share only the positive aspects of retreats.) She said that in the following days she had gained some victory over these negative feelings. I found her after the service and said I wanted to comment on what she'd said. "I know, I know," she said, before I could go on, "I can't be ruled by my feelings." I'd wanted somehow to accept her in recognizing her negative feelings and being willing to share them. She hardly heard me, so settled in her mind was her conviction that they were wrong.

If we don't treat feelings gently in our Monday through Saturday relationships with believers, worship on Sunday won't be as genuine and fulfilling as possible. Sometimes we can be so conscious of negative feelings in relationships that it's difficult to turn our attention to God. Sometimes worship becomes an emotional outlet because feelings have been closeted all week. We've coped with them poorly among ourselves and been buffeted by our work or school or neighborhood. If we have emotion in worship, let it be purely for God's praise, not to release pent-up, scrambled emotions left over from the rest of the week.

Small heavens on earth are created by imaginative, thoughtful regard for the feelings of others. We can enter into this creativity when we're at peace inside ourselves, having "owned" and cared for our personal feelings as well. Our pastor calls these small heavens "pockets of *shalom*." Let them come into being every time believers are together, two or more in Jesus' name.

Notes

1. Elizabeth O'Connor, *Journey Inward, Journey Outward* (New York: Harper & Row, 1968) p. 7.

2. *Ibid.*, p. 12.

Feelings in the Church

Feelings in the Family 8

Our church offered a mini-course on how to be more helpful in our relationships with people. Soon afterward, our ten-year-old son stormed into the house, furious and close to tears. My normal reaction would have been, "Hey, cool it," or "That's no way to behave," but I managed to say, "Wow, you're really angry."

"I'll say I am," he said with his fists clenched.

"I've hardly ever seen you so angry."

"That Gary called me a white patty."

"What'd you call him?"

"A nigger."

He went into his bedroom and slammed the door. I managed to stifle my impulse to interfere. Ten minutes later he was in the kitchen dialing the phone. "You phoning?" I asked, no longer managing. He covered the receiver. "Yeah. I'm calling Gary. What he said wasn't so bad, and look what we've done to the black people all these years."

I know what would have happened if I'd sat in judgment on his anger. First, he'd have had my anger as well as his own and Gary's to deal with, which were already quite enough. Second, he'd have had to deal with guilt that my judgment would have caused. Third, the healthy process that carried him to an acceptable conclusion to the whole affair would have been stifled by confusion. Fourth, what took ten minutes to resolve would have taken hours, and might not have been settled at all. Interrupted relationships are often resumed in spite of hurts that are never really taken care of, but the friendships become less rewarding.

Families are the cradles of feelings. In families, feelings are nurtured, and there we learn our earliest habits of hiding or being open about how we feel. In families we quickly find out which feelings to shove in the closet and which ones we can comfortably express. Little children learn fast which behaviors set them up as darlings and which bring calamity about their ears. These behavior patterns are largely the result of how their parents have accepted or rejected their honest expressions of feelings. What goes on behind the closed doors of our homes is the most telling story of what we do with feelings.

Home is the place we want to feel most comfortable and appreciated. We want to be free to be ourselves. For many, Christians among them, home is a place of disillusionment and discomfort. In fact, Christians have often added to, rather than subtracted from, the difficulties of family living, because the open, honest handling of feelings has brought antagonism rather than affection.

Why have Christians erred in this? Probably because of the high standards and expectations we set for ourselves and other family members. We think we need to attain perfection. We set goals somewhat unconsciously, in the same performance-oriented spirit that keeps us from being genuine about our inadequacies. We set these expectations out of love, but each of us is incapable of living up to what we ask of others in the family. We feel bad when we haven't measured up. We feel worse when we're reminded of it time after time by the condemnation of silence, by implications of all kinds, by nagging, by expressed disapproval. Many years ago our oldest son said to me, "Mother, if you really believe that all things work together for good, why don't you act like it?'' My tension and worry were apparent to him.

Feelings are in the crucible in our homes. Nowhere do relationships deserve more tender attention. Nowhere are the rewards sweeter when we are "feeling-oriented." Nowhere are the results more devastating when we run roughshod over feelings.

Often we handle our own family members' feelings in ways that would ostracize us if we dished it out elsewhere or outrage us if we received the same treatment. It's never too late to relearn our "feeling-handling" habits, even though it's impossible to turn the clock back to correct our failures. I count heavily on God's grace for the past, and I don't do it flippantly. God intends us to *learn* to be sensitive to feelings. Love, says Solomon, covers all offenses (Proverbs 10:12), which has to include "offensive" negative feelings.

Is hate or indifference the opposite of love? There are few (if any) Christian homes where love doesn't exist, even if shot through by anger. I know no Christian homes where indifference reigns supreme, even though individuals in some families might feign indifference or have been pressed to the point of indifference. We care when things aren't going well, and that's hopeful.

When family members are sensitive to each others' feelings, good things happen. Building an accepting atmosphere is a process. It's first a matter of thoughtful listening for what the other is feeling, an activity many view with distaste. We don't have patience with this "hearing" because as often as not it involves listening to negative feelings. We don't like our own negative feelings and we dislike them even more in our children. Sometimes listening calls for sacrifice of time and the setting aside of other pursuits, however legitimate. But we can learn to listen. The earlier we begin to listen carefully (which really boils down to showing courtesy), the happier and more relaxed our family life will be.

Try to put yourself in the shoes of your partner or child or mother or father. How would you feel if you were in the situation where trouble has developed? The Golden Rule works. Trouble at work, home, or school isn't hard to spot if you're on the lookout for feelings: irritation, discontent, indifference leading to withdrawal or depression, or just not coping. We can act toward troubled family members the way we'd like them to behave toward us if we were in their position, with understanding, respecting their privacy, offering a listening ear, getting clarification, being supportive, supplementing with help when necessary.

To give to a family member in fantasy what you can't give in fact is a "feeling" act. Dr. Norman Wright suggested this once in a lecture. What does my child or wife or husband want? Can I give it? Often such a gift doesn't cost money, but lies in the area of acceptance, praise, and support. But even if it's an impossible financial thing, I can identify with the wish itself. This granting in spirit brings feelings of warmth, caring, pleasure.

Our daughter went through about three years of desperately wanting a horse. Unwittingly, and too slowly, we came to this idea of granting it in fantasy. We wished she could have one, but we could see no practical way for it to happen. We surveyed possibilities and tried to "feel" with her about it. We never got the horse, but she worked it through. It was interesting some time later to talk to a parent whose child had had her "great horse wish" granted. She'd spent so much time with the horse that when it was time to go off to college she was incapable of relating socially and underwent a painful adjustment. I felt better about our own situation!

Not long ago, during a crisis illness in the family, I couldn't spend any time writing. It was impossible and I understood that. But the emotions I was having weren't only those of a frustrated author. Suddenly as I tried to pin down those squirming feelings, I realized that it was because I thought my husband wasn't "feeling" with me about it. When we talked and he told me he was aware of what was happening and was sorry about it, the pain was gone.

Books about family life tell you that the spirit and attitude of a family are "caught, not taught." And of course the feelings between husband and wife are home plate for this catching. When actions, not feelings, are the focus of attention, we have performance-oriented relationships. We're afraid of arousing the negative feelings of a partner for something we've done or not done. The weeds of maneuvering, secrecy, deceit begin to grow. Often our dishonesty begins over trifling things, like a little misspent money or time. If only we could be sure we'd be accepted unconditionally by our partner, including our "bad" feelings.

We fail to handle feelings well when we simplistically state, "Wives, be submissive to your husbands," and "Husbands, love your wives as Christ loved the church" (Ephesians 5:22, 23). I want to take James 3:5 and change it a bit: "How great a forest is set ablaze by those two short sentences." Whether it's from the pulpit or from Bill Gothard's "chain of command," and even when equal *time* is given to the corollary for husbands, the word comes through to the wife loudest, no doubt because that nail has been pounded longest. The woman's feelings, a master key to working this out, are scarcely considered. Even though the biblical injunction is, of course, right and good, becoming submissive can be a miserable and almost impossible experience. Feelings abound: dissatisfaction, dismay, resentment, being trapped, depression. The more desirous a wife is to be godly and thus obedient, the less she is free to deal with such negative feelings. To experience these emotions, much less to express them, is defeating. Have you ever *felt* Archie Bunker yell, "Stifle!"?

Of course in our culture the feelings of "stifle" are experienced both by wives and husbands, and they lap over into Christian families. These feelings are the opposite of encouragement. The more one is threatened, the harder it is to change. If either partner feels that love is based on performance, threat is present. If love is unconditional, we're "freed up" to perform. "There is a story of a housewife who related that her husband's love seemed to be conditioned on her keeping the house tidy and in order at all times. She maintained that she needed to know that he loved her ... in order to have the strength to keep the house clean."[1]

Several things seem evident about submission. One is that a woman who urges submissiveness upon other women is often either fulfilled in her daily life and (I'm guessing) seldom required to submit in anything distasteful to her, or else in reality she runs her husband's life. To verbalize submissiveness can take the place of putting it into practice. To demand of others what we're not required to do in our own situation is fairly common sinful behavior.

Another problem is that we speak of submissiveness and the "biblical woman," but seldom grant to women the opportunity to find their role through the women of the Bible. Except for the Jezebels we tend to honor them all, even with their mistakes. I can think of no heroines in Scripture who didn't possess a certain freedom. They had individuality, made decisions, were bold in carrying them out, and took all kinds of initiative within their circumstances: Sarah, Abigail, the Shunammite, Naomi and Ruth, Lydia, Priscilla. The "proverbial woman" seems to have run a small empire (Proverbs 31:10-31).

Mary was a woman whose individuality we underestimate. Jesus was not conceived in the womb of a timid, self-effacing Galilean girl (Luke 1:46-55). The Magnificat "... betrays a boldness that makes Mary seem almost like an Israeli *sabra* (youth) of today. This young girl was apparently voicing the same kind of rebellious patriotic fervor that erupted ten years later in the revolt of Judas of Galilee."[2] Sherwood Wirt called Mary "a Zealot and a 'prophetess' who knew that ... the 'system' had to go." We may disagree, but there's no doubt that our heavy spiritualization of the Magnificat has robbed us of some of Mary's human spirit.

Third, the command to the wife is coupled in Scripture with the assumption that submission to her husband is a reflection of the church being subject to Christ. But Jesus won the right to expect submission by demonstrating his concern for the well-being of the church by his own perfect obedience, even to death. Jesus literally put himself in every person's place. Is a husband, in a thoughtful sense, willing to "become a wife," to try feeling how she feels? Jesus entirely felt how we feel. Perhaps the husbands who best know the feelings of their wives are those who've tried most diligently to follow Christ in submission to God's will.

No wonder husbands have trouble with their half of the arrangement. Jesus loves the church in spite of her poor performance, even her infidelity to him. Why hasn't he cracked his church over the head? What is this longsuffering of his? Could Christ's example mean that a husband must learn willingly to accept whatever his wife is and does that falls short of his (or her) expectations—in the house, with the children, with finances, at church, with their friends, with business associates? Perhaps he'll need to work through her attraction to another man (though in our culture it's most often the other way around). Perhaps he'll need to back away from that attitude of possessiveness (or whatever) that assures him he always knows what she wants and what is best for her. He may have to let her explore various avenues of fulfillment: new friendships, academic or artistic interests, some activity that ignites a new spark for living. He may even lovingly have to pick up some pieces while she's learning these new things. He can't say, "I told you so," or "You should have listened to me in the first place." He isn't to be the instrument for changing her except by his fundamental love for her. No matter how we press the husband/wife-Christ/church analogy, a husband isn't God and he isn't to maneuver or manipulate his wife into his will.

To be a submissive wife is not to be nothing, yet wives do have troubled feelings about "being nothing." It takes first-rate intelligence to run a home and family, but housework hardly provides sustenance for a mind hungry for stimulating ideas, eager to take its place in a lively adult world. For whatever reasons, the majority voice in the church seems to be that women must somehow park their minds next to their makeup and satisfy their husbands as enticing enchantresses.

Is it possible that I'm doing husbands an injustice? Occasionally a husband feels the need for a wife who likes to think. Occasionally a husband isn't threatened when his wife does think. Occasionally a husband is glad if at the end of the day his wife has had enough satisfactions already in the adult world that she isn't totally dependent on him for everything she needs, emotionally, mentally, and physically. Occasionally a husband understands the feelings of his wife, and is willing to help her find her own way to achieve the intellectual and emotional satisfaction she needs. I am thankful to have such a husband.

Yet no privileges for women feel good unless they are privileges under control. Wives can just as miserably fail to appreciate the feelings a husband has in his world: feelings of insecurity, boredom, tension, inadequacy, competition. Unless these feelings are accepted at home, the feelings that lead to happy, shared, fulfilled husband/wife oneness will elude us. Few husbands have enough comfortable identification with people in a given day. It's easy for either a husband or a wife to underestimate the contribution the other makes in a job outside the home, and this misunderstanding is always communicated to the other in some more or less careless way.

This subject is important because mutual appreciation sets the "feeling tone" in our homes. Discussion of the role of women in the church certainly overlaps into this "feeling" area at home. Given the already "aggressive" American woman, the drive for women's liberation, and men running scared or putting their foot down all over the landscape like Paul Bunyan, I'm sure there will be some heated discussions within earshot of family members. Just talking about sexism triggers all sorts of feelings. There will be perplexity and frustration for both men and women as we seek biblical answers. Will we be consistent in handling our interpretation of the Jewish cultural rules for women of the first-century church? Is it certain that most of the spiritual gifts listed in Scripture were given primarily to guide men? Will we as a church do the customary thing and simply lag behind the rest of our culture as we tackle the sexism issue? We shouldn't be satisfied with the same answers our culture comes up with; we're called on to find our own solutions. If the church doesn't do its own clear thinking, we'll end up either adopting our culture's patterns or in reaction putting women farther into the background.

Perhaps the best course of all is to approach this feeling-loaded subject using the word *people* and talking about our common need to be submissive. This, after all, was Paul's approach to male-female relationships: "Be subject to one another out of reverence for Christ" (Ephesians 5:21). One of the challenges in coming into the experience of submission is that it takes courage and strength to submit ourselves to God and to one another. True submission isn't weakness. It produces, finally, the "peaceable fruit of righteousness" and is a beautiful quality of life.

A friend read some early chapters of this book and asked, "Does passion, the ability to feel deeply, get a word?" It should, beginning here with husbands and wives. Passion is an almost overwhelming thing—nothing is more consuming. To be consumed by it in the form of sexual love carries its own ecstasy. To be overwhelmed by it when it is anger can be used by God to purify. Passion is a feeling worth having.

I wonder how often Christians can "let loose" and experience it. It's often easier to cover over areas that could give rise to passion. One can set up patterns of handling deep feelings that produce polite and workable behaviors, but end by leaving feelings watered-down, insipid, weak. In the school where we learn to repress or bury feelings, the diploma is emotional sterility between husband and wife.

Of course passion is more than an emotion related to partners and sex. We feel it in other situations in our lives that awaken us or stir us deeply. We speak of the passion of Jesus. My husband suggested that this involved, increasingly as the hours wore on, his feelings about all the experiences that led him step by step through those awful last days to the cross. Perhaps the passion began when "he steadfastly set his face to go to Jerusalem" (Luke 9:51 KJV). No other human will know that depth of passion. But reduced, it is a feeling any family member can have.

It is within our own families that passions are most frequently exhibited, or the results of them most evident, causing the most blessing or damage. Obviously they can be damaging. Passion is always an intense feeling demanding significant amounts of time and energy, whether it is expressed or withheld. Sometimes the real values of passion aren't equal to the pressures of the demands it makes. Queen Orual, of C. S. Lewis's *Till We Have Faces,* speaking of a passion of her own, remarks "how suddenly a passion which has for years been wrapped round the whole heart will dry up and wither. Perhaps in the soul, as in the soil, these growths that show the brightest colours and put forth the most overpowering smell have not always the deepest root."[3] Whether passion takes a negative turn ("I hate her with a passion") or a positive one ("He is passionately involved in the fight against cancer"), it can get us into difficulty. Hate can lead to violence; positive involvement can cause a person to neglect family and friends. So passions must, of all emotions, be heard honestly and handled well. Knowing how to take care of less stormy feelings prepares us for the infrequent ones of passion when they come, allowing those with redemptive and fulfilling qualities to be fully experienced, being able to overcome those that are unholy.

There are lessons about feelings to be learned from children. When we have become, as Jesus suggested, like little ones, we will have learned a great deal. A three-year-old friend of ours was with me on some errands, including an overlong piece of business in a bank. When we left, I was pleased to accept a big red balloon from the receptionist as a reward for his patience. He seemed pleased, too, at first, but in the car he put it gingerly on the seat between us. "It squeaks when I hold it," he said. When we got home, he politely declined to take it in. "It might break." Here was a child with well-defined feelings about balloons.

As I thought about it later, and reviewed our own family's "balloon days," I realized we'd seldom had a wholly pleasant balloon experience. Balloons squeak, bang, leak, and float away. Adults tend to forget the poignant feelings associated with balloons and other unreliable things—like broken promises and unfulfilled plans.

When Jesus pointed us to children for our example, it wasn't only because of their trust and responsiveness, nor their dependence and neediness. It was also because of their inbuilt honesty about feelings. And Jesus inserted the word *little* with good reason. Children soon learn to hide how they feel in order to please the people they're dependent on. I suppose there aren't many three-year-olds who haven't already lost some of this honesty.

It is perhaps too simple an illustration to build on, but the little boy I have described brought several points home to me. He understood himself and his feelings. He thought of his own feelings first. He expressed himself without being anxious about my response. He knew his capabilities; he refused to be burdened with something he couldn't handle.

I accepted it all without comment and with cheerfulness, partly because he belonged to someone else and I didn't feel responsible in that area. How easily I could have muddled his feelings. "But Jesse, the nice lady gave it to you!" "I think you ought to show it to your mommy and daddy." "Are you sure you don't want it?" How many times does something not really matter, but in blowing it up, like the balloon, we infuse it with anxiety and guilt.

The guarded and watchful (or overt and aggressive) behavior of children whose parents are not "feeling-oriented" shows early in their response to the larger world. Ironically, because the world is so fraught with dangers to feelings, the child who has been taught to hide and maneuver emotions is often saved the painful experiences of those who have learned to be honest and to trust in a reliable response. But honesty and trust are basic to growth in God, who is always reliable, so they are worth the cost.

Between childhood and adulthood lies mysterious and exciting adolescence. Dr. James Oraker points out "major shifts in the three areas of sex, intellect, and identity which are unique to the adolescent."[4] He defines the sexual change as "perhaps the most dramatic ... with emotional overtones." The intellectual change creeps up less noticeably. "Parents who have consistently exercised tight control over their children can be completely blind to the onset of the intellectual change." Dr. Oraker suggests that the shift in identity ("Who am I?") is in our culture no longer so much a matter of "What will I do when I finish my training?" as of "Who am I in relationships?" These adolescent "shifts" all involve feelings. In the struggling times, parents feel alarmed, edgy, perplexed, disappointed, helpless. The adolescent feels mixed-up, forlorn, disdainful, resentful, bitter.

Listening to feelings pays off. If we have older children who haven't been allowed the privilege of "owning" angers and hurts, it takes awhile to encourage them.

"Something seems to be bothering you."

"Well, yes."

"Do you want to share it?"

Silence. "You won't like it."

"Perhaps you're afraid I'll be disappointed or angry."

More silence. "You're right. I don't think you'll like it."

"You'll never know until you say it."

"OK. Well..." and out it comes.

This kind of conversation doesn't take place on the run. Nor is the atmosphere that leads to silence or reproof about negatives the kind that encourages an adolescent or child to share happy feelings.

My husband and I listened to a lot of feelings as one of our daughters thought through the matter of dating. She knew how we felt. At sixteen is there anything new a parent can communicate about convictions and feelings? We've watched some parents guide their children through the teens successfully. Usually their guidance wasn't based on rules, but on lots of trust and warmth. The successful alternative to "guidance based on rules" takes more time than laying down laws, but it eliminates the anxiety and strain of watching to see if rules are kept and punishing if they aren't. We need willingness to listen intelligently, to try to understand, to talk things out, and then honestly to evaluate our adult feelings in privacy.

It's much easier to say, for instance, "No dating until you're sixteen," than it is to raise a child whose discretion and judgment you can trust about places to go, hours to keep, sexual pressures to cope with. Of course these kinds of choices start years before. It's helpful for children to be allowed to choose all along the way when alternatives are actually possible and a choice can be freely granted. The choices will differ from family to family, but reasonable choices always give a child or adolescent a feeling of personal worth and integrity ("You have good things inside you that we can trust").

Of course different families will also have their own rules. It's true that adolescents need limits and are often grateful for them; limits can evoke feelings of security and relief. "Feeling-oriented" parents can sense when limits need to be set, and they can also be flexible and move toward more freedom. "As the child becomes more capable of making responsible choices, the parents can change their style of decision-making."[5]

As in other areas, feelings must be "heard," admitted, and handled in family life. Adults and children can learn that "hearing" what goes on inside doesn't always need to be verbalized. It's hard for children who have been "feeling-aware" to meet a hostile world, but wisdom learned in handling feelings inside their homes and inside themselves will help them adjust outside the family and help them build other relationships. It's essential for a child to know there is a safe and acceptable place to express feelings.

But having established that as a working principle, it's also important to know that family feelings flying around like bullets can do damage, even when they're accepted and understood. I have waited to say this, because usually we err on the side of closeting our feelings. Not long ago I was tired after cooking dinner. I had made something new, and as usual had in mind the general happiness of those who would be at dinner. One of the younger generation bounced into the kitchen and said, "What's for dinner? Oh. Ugh." Later I explained how bad that had made me feel at that moment, and invited my child to feel "Ugh" if need be, but to forego saying it. Since our family is learning to be sensitive about feelings, I got a positive response.

Parents who allow children uncontrolled expression of feelings in the cause of openness and honesty can take a lot of punishment in return for their love. And later, it's hard for those children to learn that not all adults will respond like sponges. They'll learn, but it would be easier to learn at home.

When our feelings are well cared for at home, we can sally forth with confidence into the world, a world that continually reflects sin and sorrow. At least there is a haven to go back to or to remember. Helped with feelings at home, we are much healthier members of the body of Christ. We are more ready to take risks, and we are more open to pain. We are becoming like Jesus.

Notes

1. John Powell, *The Secret of Staying in Love* (Niles, Illinois: Argus Communications, 1974) p. 51.

2. Sherwood E. Wirt, *Social Conscience of the Evangelical* (New York: Harper & Row, 1968) p. 13.

3. C. S. Lewis, *Till We Have Faces* (Grand Rapids, Michigan: William B. Eerdmans Publishing Co., 1956) p. 267.

4. James Oraker, "The Adolescent Family: A Time For New Commitment," *Theology News and Notes,* Vo. XX No. 4, p. 9.

5. *Ibid.*

Feelings and Counsel- ing 9

We all are apprehensive at times. Is this job I've accepted the right one? Is the gas going to hold out through this long, empty stretch? Is this rock too high to dive from? I remember an awful apprehension when I swam across a small bay and got near the point of no return—had I misjudged the distance? Verging on an unknown makes us apprehensive, and I think apprehension is the right word to describe the reaction of many Christians to counseling.

Through counseling I discovered the part feelings play in all of life. I was encouraged by a psychologist to examine my own emotions as though they really had something to tell me. I learned that understanding the state of my feelings was a way to uncover problems. This was all part of my own struggle to make life come into harmony with the biblical injunctions to mature behavior. I knew so well what I wanted to be and yet was not.

Each of us treads a different path, so my experience is uniquely my own. But as I have shared it, I've made the further discovery that there are others like me whose problems refuse, as mine refused, to go away in the face of earnest effort. There can be desperate inner turmoil, a stifling spiritual claustrophobia even while engaging in prayer, worship, and Bible study. These three activities normally produce spiritual health. Now I know that they must be accompanied by close communication with other accepting and growing believers. My thanks to all who are working to make small-group encounters effective in the church!

My husband and I certainly prayed about our difficulties, but even in the intimacy of a basically good marriage it was hard to see problems objectively, to analyze each other's behavior and motivations without more hurting than healing. I made resolves during times alone with the Lord and especially at conferences and Sunday worship "highs." Every height I reached had its corresponding level of what I judged to be failure. During a week set aside in our church, a "week of waiting on God," this pattern came to a climax for me. We sat in the sanctuary for six consecutive evenings, quietly praying or thinking. There was singing and sharing, but basically there was quietness. Surrounded by hundreds of our congregation also quiet and praying for each other, I *knew* some new thing had to happen that would change the old unconquered problems in my life.

I had grown up in a family in which the field of psychology was a respected one; my parents considered the intricacies of the human mind a legitimate study. My husband felt the same way, so we didn't have the struggle many Christians have in deciding to seek professional help. We delayed only because we thought trying harder and praying more would get us past the problems.

When I did start to explore the dilemma with a skilled person, I began to understand myself. An effective key to my new understanding was the realization that I had buried many unpleasant feelings I couldn't acknowledge as a "mature" Christian. Long years of covering problems, of putting a good face on things in spite of how I felt, hadn't paid dividends in my life. Now it took awhile to learn to listen to my feelings because it was an unfamiliar experience.

At first I was hesitant to tell anyone about this releasing adventure because of awareness that Christian friends might not understand. Some months before, a psychologist was scheduled to speak to a group at our church and I had announced my intention to hear him. A friend laughed and said, "You don't need a psychologist when you have the Bible." It's true that the Bible contains good psychology and that the roots of good psychological care are biblical, but for intricate predicaments the solutions are more difficult than simply knowing enough Scripture. We do need psychologists.

Years before, I had read everything I could find by Dr. Paul Tournier, a psychotherapist. Reading him was like finding shade on a hot day. Even then I felt a wonderful relief, knowing that a loving, gentle, knowledgeable person existed, who wasn't alarmed or judgmental when a Christian was troubled. "But Jesus is like that," you may say. A little girl complained of feeling lonely in her bedroom at night. When her father said, "But Jesus is here, Judy," she replied, "I know it, Daddy, but I want somebody with skin on." It is God's intention, part of his plan, that we get help from people with "skin on." But because Paul Tournier was in Switzerland, my contact with him had been strictly one-way.

After I had moved past the most painful part of therapy (the searching and seeing and acknowledging, the getting rid of false guilts that don't go away with confessing), I found the relief so great that to share a little of the worth of good counseling wasn't hard.

Christians are apprehensive about counseling because we would rather avoid the mystery of deeply personal inwardness. We aren't exactly sure why we should need counseling when we have good preachers and teachers. Most Christian leaders take healthy growth in the body of Christ for granted. They see themselves as passing the ball of truth to a lot of halfbacks and quarterbacks who grab it and run for touchdowns. The searching, tentative, testing-the-ground approach to Christian growth that takes place during counseling doesn't seem quite right. Counseling has been used largely for people with problems who can't manage them by themselves. But counseling is *calling forth* answers from inside out; it isn't *handing* answers from the outside in.

The fields of psychology and psychiatry generally have developed outside the Christian context, so that much of the older therapeutic philosophy cuts across the grain of biblical truth. But wariness about counseling is more than disagreement with psychology's past. It stems from the fact that many Christians still feel it's shameful to have problems one can't handle emotionally. To them, "emotional" and "spiritual" are the same thing.

The confusion of emotional disturbance with being "unspiritual" often comes out when professional psychological or psychiatric help (or even assitance from a skilled lay counselor or pastor) is suggested. Defenses are instantly up: "But I do love the Lord," or "I intend to keep praying about it," or "I've read such-and-such a book," or "I've been to this-or-that seminar." Many Christians have a hard time seeing themselves as needing specialized help. They can't accept that it's "all right" to have emotional problems. It isn't comfortable, true. But it isn't the same as saying, "I'm not right with God" or "I'm a spiritual cripple." Watching such people labor with their inward difficulties, problems that more often than not are at the "feeling" level, I am amazed at their failure to seek help. It's as though they were saying, "I think I have appendicitis, but I don't need a doctor because I love Jesus."

Another hesitation about counseling arises from the idea that it is indulgent. Counseling is not a process during which a person is comforted, reassured, and somehow relieved of accountability and responsibility. Although comfort and reassurance are fruits of counseling at its best, the opposite takes place during the counseling process. The psychologist stands as a kind of wall so that escape from one's inner turmoil is no longer possible; the alternative is to confront oneself. Slippery, spiritually correct language is no longer a hiding place. Pastors are often misled by those who *sound* most theologically healthy; people have learned how to escape by using the right phrases. In good therapy, running away is over, and therapy is sometimes discontinued by the client for that reason: the inward search is too painful.

Although the whole field of psychology is showing healthy new trends, from a Christian point of view a Christian psychologist or psychiatrist is usually most helpful for a Christian. A Christian counselor already shares a great deal of common ground with the client because they both have the mind of Christ. I was able to share my Christian experience and to discuss both the realities and the lack of reality in my relationship to God. The counselor caught me in generalizations and subtle dishonesties in my spiritual "arrivings."

My own therapy was accomplished without the Bible open in the counselor's hand. I doubt if he could have provided me with scriptural insights from any particular verses I didn't already know. I've tried to explain to people that Bible exposition isn't always necessary or even advisable in therapy, that an open Bible doesn't insure any better counseling, but this is hard for many to understand. It's ridiculous to judge whether a counselor is godly or capable on the basis of how much Scripture is used in a therapy session. The study of our minds and emotions involves more than a knowledge of the Bible. To insist on an open Bible is somewhat like not trusting a medical doctor if you don't see a Bible on his examining table, or even like not crossing a bridge unless you're sure it was designed by a Christian engineer. God is always present when Christians are together, or when truth is in operation.

A friend of ours discovered an analogy while working on a switchboard one summer. She would say, "That line is busy; I'll put you on hold." It came to her that Christians do this with God when they want to go off on their own. "Wait,

God. I'll put you on hold and get back to you soon." Going to see a competent psychologist isn't like that. God doesn't sit back while the therapist takes over where he has failed. God is active in any healing process. If it *is* true healing, God is active in it even if he isn't recognized.

Not everyone with a good grasp of Scripture is qualified to counsel. The idea that anyone can counsel not only nullifies the usefulness of learned skills, but also leaves out the calling of God to a ministry of counseling based on his gift-giving. Some feel that all Bible-knowledgeable Christians who are "right with God" can confront people who have problems, warning and admonishing them by the use of Scripture. The main thrust of this technique is to find some sin behind the problem and to bring about repentance as a basis for the solution.[1] I've often felt, in the warmth of the body of Christ, an awakening dash of cold water from Scripture that has brought new direction. But when a person is troubled and perplexed, this kind of head-on confrontation can be destructive. It's no way to find a solution to those heavy-treading ghosts of false guilts which so many Christians have in their lives. It's no way to provide release for one whose difficulties stem primarily from the sin of others, even though each of us is responsible before God to seek release. It's no way to call forth the only kind of change that lasts, from the inside out. It discourages the sharing of needs because in such an atmosphere there's a hint of shame in opening oneself to reveal "bad" things. This kind of confrontation is based on the assumption that feelings are not significant in problem solving.

I worked at this kind of "counseling" for many years. As a pastor's wife I would listen and immediately begin to fasten on the sin I thought was behind the problem. Kindly and in what I hoped came across in a loving way, I would point it out. I repeated Scripture to those who already knew it well enough. What they really needed was an accepting atmosphere in which they could view themselves as worthwhile and relax enough to hear what was going on inside.

Long ago I talked frequently with a friend about her difficult husband. I would keep pointing out her failure, reasoning to myself that to agree with her would only confirm her in her own opinions. The husband wasn't around to be preached at and she was—right there in front of me to hear her half of the sins! One day she burst into tears, saying I never took her part, and she didn't bring up the subject again. She needed neither "preaching" nor someone to take her part, but an open, judgment-free presence in which to think and explore. The Holy Spirit was in her to convict her of sin. I didn't need to try. Basically this woman wanted to please God. Generally all children want to please their parents, and sincere Christians are no different in wanting to please their heavenly Father. Children and adults alike want to be trusted as reliable people. With the self-condemnation so common to perplexed adult Christians, this principle of an accepting atmosphere is important to cultivate. It is the aura, the fragrance, that surrounded Jesus. When earnest Christians are deeply troubled and can't identify the source, judgmental confrontation invariably produces more panic and increases despair.

Tournier says, "The virtue of psychotherapy is the virtue of non-judgment. We are overwhelmed by it and overjoyed, every time that we experience it afresh. We see in it a sign of God's grace."[2] I would think Tournier overstated his case if I hadn't experienced this good grace of God in a therapist's office myself.

At the beginning of the chapter, I touched on the misunderstanding many have about how people change. A great difference exists between *telling* someone how they ought to behave based on biblical commands (as in preaching and giving advice), and *helping* them to see a clear way to change behavior in light of the same biblical imperatives. Giving advice is often fruitless because of a subtle implied judgment: "I need to tell you because you aren't capable of knowing what is best."

The church will always need preaching, the giving forth of truth—it is one of God's special gifts to some of his servants. But often people already know truth that is not operative in their lives. Telling them again can confirm and strengthen but it doesn't always produce change and growth. Frequently when people have heard a strong preacher or lecturer or have been in the presence of a firm Bible study leader, they have no question about what is true, but their problems have become heavier and harder to solve because of pressure from outside in. There is no opportunity to step back, to look inward, to discover what keeps change from taking place. Often troubled people can come away from a doctrinally sound leader feeling reinforced for a few hours, but it doesn't last. When they've been alone long enough to lose the flavor of that strong person, to find themselves on their own again, the problems, the depression, or even despair are as overwhelming as ever. Sheep are sometimes led and sometimes driven; "driving" seems the most obvious, direct, and sensible way to get people moving for God, but gently leading them is often more effective. The Bible study leader who said, "If he wants a counselor to tell him what I've already told him, let him go to one," simply misunderstood what counseling is.

There ought to be a word here in behalf of good teaching, a gift lying somewhere between preaching and counseling. Teaching should be a time when the inward look is an active process. "And the teacher, whoever he is, ought not to be a man of answers but a man of questions. 'Who do men say that I am? Who do you say that I am?' "[3] It feels good to be in the presence of someone who invites questions. For a teacher to be questioned in such a way shows that something worthwhile is going on within the person who is being taught.

The process of healing of the mind and emotions is often very slow. It involves unlearning many years of thought and behavior patterns that may have been "caught" in childhood from parents who weren't in touch with themselves as individuals or with each other. The unlearning must be accompanied by developing new skills in handling ourselves. I am reminded of the critical physical shape many people are in when they finally get to the physician at mission hospitals, some beyond healing. There are people who have neglected emotional health until the cure is not only long and complex, but never finally accomplished.

In skilled counseling "an ounce of prevention is worth a pound of cure." A great deal of understanding can be gained when difficulties seem minor but persistent, and a great deal of trouble, including physical illness, can be avoided later. Counseling provides tools for handling all of life in a more mature way. One of the bonuses I received from therapy is the use of these tools ever since. When I became aware of my feelings, I discovered reasons for restlessness, or lack of peace, or depression, or a shortage of the spice of life.

For example, I recall the first time I began to do "alone" essentially what I had learned to do in therapy. I had gradually become aware of a vague sense of dissatisfaction and I started consciously to locate the reason. (To look inward is not to say I sat with my head in my hands, for they were very busy days.) When I could, I took time to look into myself until a new insight came to me. With the beginning of a summer full of family pressures, I wouldn't see so much of my husband alone. Time alone together had become very important to me.

God intends to use all kinds of people in our lives, showing us our dependence on each other. Evangelical Christians are especially encouraged to "go straight to God" with a problem. Unaided, this can be a lonely experience. In spite of heavy emphasis on the need to spend time apart with God, Protestant Christians aren't trained in the art of experiencing God alone. In the healing of emotions or feelings, God uses pastors, friends, the Bible, worship experiences, good books, as well as skilled lay and professional counselors. He wants to use wives with their husbands and husbands with their wives. God certainly gives us direct answers, one to one, but he often strengthens his people on earth by making us dependent on each other, including dependence on one another's prayers. This increases our understanding of each other, as well as our understanding of ourselves, and helps us to wholeness.

If all Christians were instructed and encouraged to be more feeling-oriented in living out life, there would be a good deal less need for skilled counseling. But as long as we are here, waiting for Jesus to come, professional and amateur counselors, called by God to use their unique gifts, are among his choice servants. And problems aren't merely hindrances on the horizons of God's people. They are opportunities for expanding our worlds, for seeing new truths about people, for learning faster and better the depth of the love of God in Jesus Christ.

Notes

1. This approach to therapy is developed by Dr. Jay Adams in his book *Competent to Counsel* (Nutley, N.J.: Presbyterian and Reformed Publishing Co., 1970).

2. Paul Tournier, *Guilt and Grace*, p. 102.

3. Elizabeth O'Connor, *Journey Inward, Journey Outward*, p. 13.

Some Specifics of Handling Feelings

10

I feel hesitant and cautious as I begin to write more specifically about handling feelings. I want to say only true and workable things. I've been thinking and writing for three or four hours. I'm aware of annoyance when I'm interrupted. The annoyance is followed by feelings of guilt if the interruption is legitimate and I haven't responded well. If I'm patient and feel respect toward my ''interrupter'' I feel all right. Right now, this is my own personal feeling "mix." At any given moment everyone is involved with feelings, with what goes on inside. Everyone is constantly, more or less consciously, burying, pushing back, or taking good care of feelings.

In the book thus far I've talked about feelings in the major areas of life where I personally feel them. Generally they are areas where everyone deals with feelings, though perhaps relatively few share the experience of the counseling process. I wrote a long chapter titled "Feelings and the Mission of the Church." I felt unsettled about it and a friend said, "That doesn't lie in the area of your personal experience, does it?" He knew I'd had no need to work through feelings in another culture. I left that chapter out of the book.

Each of us is involved in different "feeling" experiences. Many of you spend perhaps a third or more of your time where my life doesn't touch yours: at school or in employment outside your home. These are major arenas of life—hard, unyielding, unfeeling arenas.

Not only is each person's "feeling" experience unique, but not everyone is at the same level of growth in "feeling awareness." There is a wide range of emotional health. Our behavior reflects how well we handle feelings. Some people are simply withdrawn. At the other extreme are people who are aggressive in a way that comes through as lacking control. In either case, feelings aren't "controlled" well. Most behavior falls somewhere between the extremes of this wide range. Other people are aware of their feelings and are deeply "congruent." That is, they agree with themselves inside. They are not warring within. Their behavior is in tune with and comes out of inner unity. We observe that this behavior is consistent with what they say. We see that it is behavior appropriate to each situation. Moreover, we see it as behavior which somehow reflects the behavior of Jesus, a beautiful and desirable goal. As we learn to be in touch with our feelings and handle them well, we move toward this goal. If you can think of any way in which your behavior doesn't have these qualities, you have some learning and practicing to do.

In spite of our personal uniqueness and different levels of growth, there is a commonality about feelings and our handling of them that knows no boundaries of vocation or lot in life. Three facts about emotions have begun to clarify for me as I've kept trying to learn to handle them.

One fact is that we must strike a balance between the universality of "feeling" experiences (because they're part of being human), and the individuality of each person. The more I'm aware of my own feelings, the more I sense how others feel. At the same time there comes over me a stand-off respect for the privacy of others. I can never feel for others. I must exercise my imagination and try to feel what someone else is feeling so I can make some kind of identification with that person, but I cannot actually know another's heights or depths. Above all I can't suggest by word or by attitude what is right or wrong to others about their feelings. The spirit of judgment is always to be avoided, but particularly judgment on how someone feels. There is no sin in feeling one way or another, and judgment deals with sin. I am not God to anyone at any time, and neither are you. This applies to self-judgment as well; you are not God to yourself. And to say this is far from experiencing it. Work at it, and you will discover you are a hairsbreadth from judging feelings.

The judgment is subtle. For example, a person has a serious illness, which, without God's direct intervention, will lead to physical death. Over and over someone will say to this person, "You must have faith." What it really sounds like is, "If you have enough faith, you will be healed; if you aren't healing, you have sin in your life." It feels like judgment. Since most people really do care, one layer down, what they are *really* saying is, "Look. I'm sorry you're sick. But I can't handle—I don't even want to think about—the terrible things you must be feeling. I'm afraid you can't handle those feelings either. So have faith." It's exactly the principle James brings out in his letter: "If a brother or sister is ill-clad and in lack of daily food, and one of you says to them, 'Go in peace, be warmed and filled,' without giving them the things needed for the body, what does it profit?" (2:16). The response to difficult things like illness would be much more like emotional food and clothes if one could say, "That must be very hard. You must be feeling some very heavy things." This kind of attitude brings inner healing of spirit. The comfort of 2 Corinthians 1:3, 4 certainly begins with empathy. There is freedom in this kind of response that lets us go on to *do* good things for people who are hurting: notes, gifts, reassurances of all kinds. A truly empathetic person usually doesn't fade out of the picture when the going gets rough. When one believer says to another, "Whatever you're feeling is all right," it is a small copy of

God's reassurance, and helps us to experience his love.

Another fact about emotions is that always wanting to feel good is dangerous. Yet who, except in a neurotic sense, would choose to feel bad? The danger is that we are so quick to manipulate our emotions and circumstances to keep on feeling good. As I've worked out from my own inner difficulties, caused in large part by poor handling of feelings, with mysterious and uncongealed hope I expected the light to dawn one morning and to find all trouble gone. All that dawned were new and difficult things to handle. But I realized the new difficulties were more often from without than from within. In fact, as we become orderly inside, in touch with ourselves, we are increasingly aware of trouble from without.

Heaven will not come to us on earth; why should the servant be above the Master? But the lowest aspirations we have toward heaven are based on the fact that there we will no longer feel bad. We are betrayed into a false hope for a steady state of feeling good on earth. Our affluence calls us to keep on feeling good. Comfortable things of earth are indispensable for this: heat in cold, coolness in heat, food in the freezer, digestive helps on the bathroom shelf, and so on. We are also betrayed by a weak theology which reaches out for "spiritual" good feelings; perhaps the more exotic gifts of the Holy Spirit will do it. If we pursue "spiritual" manifestations hard enough, we will feel good. That is, we will be above the dust and dirt of problems. If we had God's *very* best we wouldn't be plagued.

Jesus demonstrated the opposite. One day he had sent the disciples across the Sea of Galilee in a boat while he remained behind on land to pray (Mark 6:45-51). "And he saw that they were distressed in rowing, for the wind was against them." That's just the way it is when you row against the wind—it's distressing. Jesus had no intention of easing their discomfort except by not adding his weight to the boat. Hours later he walked on the water, intending to pass by them. It was their terror (caused by superstition) that compelled his attention. We know distress far more often than we know terror, and he evidently expects us to cope with the distress. His Holy Spirit will never leave us nor forsake us, but he did say, "In the world you will have trouble."

Now someone may think, "If I learn to handle feelings well, that will be the answer to my search for fulfillment: I will feel fine." But feelings worked at only become clarified. Positive feelings feel better, but the negatives feel worse. Satisfaction, gladness, yearning, anticipation, reluctance, indifference, dismay, and anger feel more and more like themselves. Feelings are to be felt, more keenly in both directions. Count on it.

Another fact about emotions is that often we are helped in our growth by a model. Jesus is the best model. Though God, he was fully human. He was moved with pity; his friends wanted to remove him from the crowd because something about his exhaustion made them say, "He is beside himself"; he marveled because of the unbelief of those in Nazareth; he said, "Come away by yourselves and rest awhile" because he knew how it felt to be weary; he had compassion on a great throng because they were as sheep without a shepherd; he healed a deaf man aside from the multitude privately, perhaps because he was sensitive about this man's need—so the first sounds he heard wouldn't be a traumatically loud noise; he had compassion on the crowd because they had nothing to eat; when the Pharisees pressed him, he sighed deeply in his spirit; he was indignant when the disciples rebuked the children. What feelings were his as he headed for Jerusalem that last time so that Mark said, "They were amazed, and those who followed were afraid." Yet under the fearful pressure of all he knew awaited him in Jerusalem, he cared for a dirty, blind, smelly beggar. The last week of his life, we read that he "fell to the ground" in Gethsemane. The word has the sense of throwing himself down, of desperation, even of writhing. Later "the chief priests accused him of many things." How awful it feels to be accused of even one thing.

When I try to think of exactly how feelings are to be handled, what comes immediately to my mind is a large reservoir, a dam, powerfully full. The potential for directed energy is immense, and so is the potential for disaster. Effective controls are built into the massive wall that holds the power back. In earlier chapters I have suggested three controls to help us handle the reservoir of our emotions, three steps we can take to good handling of feelings: (1) listening/ recognizing/ labeling; (2) acknowledging/ admitting/ accepting; (3) deciding/ choosing a way/ acting. I will develop these somewhat. But the thought of that big reservoir, the depth of it, the potential of it, is awesome. No one can prescribe "the way" to handle feelings. I have been learning to practice the above principles for some months, and it is partly out of my own experience that I can be more specific. Talking with others brings additional insight. But the steps are more like climbing a mountain path with twists and turns, with ups and downs, than going upstairs from one level to another.

Listening/ Recognizing/ Labeling

Have you begun to listen to yourself? Have you been trying to label what you're feeling? We learn most worthwhile things only by doing them: praying, studying, handling finances, speed-reading, and so on. Similarly, we learn to handle feelings only by working at it. It takes time. It can hurt. The simple list of feeling words at the end of this chapter will alert you to the fact that there are thousands of words in our vocabulary that can be used to express feeling states.

1) Remember that "positive" and "negative" mean feeling good or bad, *not* "right" or "wrong." Try substituting "happy" and "unhappy" for positive and negative.

2) Notice degrees or intensities of feelings, and make sure a feeling word is appropriate to the depth of a particular experience.

3) If you disagree with where some words are listed, you are on the right track! Feeling words can go in any category you wish. Feelings are only tools and they are yours to use. Just be sure you communicate clearly with yourself and others.

4) Remember that the few words listed are only to awaken your imagination. Listen to Bilbo Baggins: "I feel all thin, sort of *stretched,* ... like butter that has been spread over too much bread."[1]

5) Some feeling words are big umbrellas that can be simply convenient or become something to hide under. Beware of terrific, wonderful, great, fine, terrible, awful.

6) It is interesting to realize there are at least three times as many negative as positive feeling words. We can safely assume that we have lots of negative feelings to handle.

I call listening the "first giant step." While learning, it's the most time-consuming part of the process. Of course, you must associate a "why" with the feelings you are pinning down. It is one thing to label anger, or fear, or frustration and another thing to clearly identify the reason for it. Sometimes the "why" or "whys" are quickly obvious. Sometimes, particularly when the "why" is involved with intimate relationships or matters which are personally vital, we are somewhat reluctant to clarify the reason for negative feelings. It is seldom necessary or desirable to label the "whys" of our happier emotions—they aren't associated with the need to solve problems, and happiness is perhaps best experienced without analysis! To list unhappy feelings on paper, and write out the "whys" next to them gets them out there where we can look at them, and the longer we put off this process the more extensive the list becomes. Without the "why" the next step of acknowledging is only half effective, and the last step of decision-making is hardly possible at all.

Begin by listening to what you're *currently* feeling. A student may be feeling frustration or panic over exams and papers, or feelings of relief and reward because these things are done. An employee may be feeling indignant or jealous because a promotion has come to someone who doesn't seem to deserve it, or may feel elated because of commendation from a superior. Without being aware of current feelings it's more difficult to be in touch with the next layer down. There are layers of "feeling awareness." For the student, there may be general dissatisfaction with the whole educational process or a feeling of appreciation for the opportunities school affords; for the person on the job there may be deep-seated uneasiness about spending a lifetime in a particular work, or a basic feeling of well-being—having found the right niche. Another example of "awareness layers" came to me from a friend. She shared her feelings of unhappiness with the performance of other people. Not far underneath she discovered disappointment at her own abilities; she is critical with herself. No doubt with all of these examples, there are deeper layers where negatives are concerned. Bad experiences build layers of negative feelings.

As we become aware of what we're feeling, we quickly realize that some feelings are associated with minor matters, others with major situations. Not only are there awareness layers, but there are feelings that are easily handled and those that are difficult. It was a minor experience to feel irritation when I was recently held up in traffic by street construction. But it's always a major matter to start getting in touch with feelings about one's marriage. When dullness in marriage is acknowledged, the process of uncovering the layers (the "whys" revealed by discovering our feelings), becomes a major effort.

An active, persistent desire to solve a problem, such as

may be uncovered in "the next layer down" process, is necessary to arrive at a solution. Problem solving calls for a steady will toward that goal. Some quiet hours are essential for listening. Part of a Christian's devotional life should involve this kind of time and search.

, The hearing of our own feelings can be hastened by help from someone who cares about and understands feelings. Self-disclosure is a great boost to self-awareness. If you're being "helped" by someone and the most obvious reaction you're having is a feeling of frustration, you're probably at the wrong door. I'm assuming that your known sins are confessed, and you're willing to confess and make right any other sins newly recognized during the listening and hearing process. One way to structure this self-disclosure is to have someone listen to you in a private place, without interrupting, for five minutes. You try to state your feelings as accurately as possible. Then your listener should try to restate what he or she has heard. You may discover that communication between you was unclear; you didn't state your feelings as you really felt them, or the listener didn't "hear." In any case, to clarify at that point is a helpful exercise.

If we're actively listening to and for our feelings, God brings present circumstances, memories, Scripture, relationships to bear on solutions for underlying difficulties. Recently a very big difficulty was largely resolved in my own life. The ingredients were a distinctly remembered and unhappy childhood experience; a consciousness of unease in my life in the present, which seemed related to that distant event; relationships that felt uncomfortable to me; and finally a long talk (or rather, a listen) with my daughter as she told me an experience of her own. Shortly after, and rather suddenly, something jelled inside and I had the key to my own search. "So that's what it was all about! That's no doubt the 'why' of my troubled feelings." I think it fell together because I was more or less actively working on it, praying about it sometimes, wanting an answer.

Acknowledging/ Admitting/ Accepting

Acknowledging, admitting, accepting (notice the progression) is the most valuable step. If we could have accepted ourselves in general to begin with, we wouldn't have "feeling" problems. If you feel good about life, about yourself and your relationships, acceptance is pure pleasure.

Willingness to meet *all* negative feelings without threat or fear or self-condemnation is essential. Paralysis will set in immediately after the first listening if the information you've uncovered or discovered isn't a "welcome guest" in your mind. This acknowledgment frees us to make decisions. I don't have to slow up the process, the approaching solution, with feelings of guilt. The more quickly we can accept what we hear, the more will be revealed to us. If we turn aside in nonacceptance, we simply block the way to further progress.

Since I'm dependent on a process over which I don't have all the control (the reservoir is deep, much of it below the level of our consciousness), acceptance allows me to relax, to be unhurried. Life is too pressing always to hold these negative feelings and unsolved puzzles in conscious tension. If we have accepted them, yet can't immediately discover all we need to know about them, we can learn to wait. I've discovered that my mind has a kind of shelf on which I can lay unsolved problems. I think a principle exists within us that tends toward healing if we don't fight it with nonacceptance, and the healing process continues in between our active efforts to seek solutions.

Acceptance of negatives is hard and will be further discussed in chapter 12. I will share an experience of my own that is difficult to disclose because I'm still working through the terrible feelings it brought. In a class at church we were led through the last night of Jesus' life, from his first trial to his crucifixion. The teacher of this class, a scientist, gave a carefully researched and unemotional step-by-step walk through those hours. Three or four times I was moved to tears, which doesn't happen to me very often. At the climax of the cross there came swiftly into my mind this thought: "I hope someone is noticing how this moves me." It makes my heart pound and my throat tighten to repeat it, so deep is my disappointment in myself. I got a glimpse of self-abhorrence. That morning I immediately thrust it aside and have kept pushing since. Perhaps right now, by writing it down, I am made to face it more fully. You think I'm making too much of it? You think I shouldn't have shared it with you? Perhaps you're thinking, "How could she?" For me to accept those feelings, an unpleasant reality about myself, isn't easy, but I'm doing it because it hasn't changed God's opinion of me at all.

Even when we approach being judgment-free, acceptance of another's pain is difficult. Dear friends of ours have a daughter who may very well have a progressive, awful disease. When her mother tells me about it, although I love her and want very much to help, I don't really want to hear. I think: "The doctors surely haven't diagnosed it correctly," or "It's obviously too soon to know," or "You must be exaggerating." I am too sensitive to feelings to say these things out loud; how terrible it would be if I did say them. Although I wouldn't be judging my friend's feelings, I would be making other judgments over which she has no control and I would only add to her pain. My problem is that I don't *want* her to feel bad, nor her husband, nor any members of her family, least of all her daughter.

Deciding/ Choosing a Way/ Acting

We sometimes find that with the step of acknowledgment and acceptance the process is complete. As I suggested earlier, nothing more may be necessary than to live with new freedom. My discoveries about myself have often in themselves been final kinds of things, not requiring decision or action. That is true of the experience I described about resolving a large difficulty. I am grateful to God.

One decision is to do nothing. Settled indecision is always a decision.

Pencil and paper help. To list possible courses of action and see them in black and white is confrontive and clarifying.

To decide well you must know what pleases God. You had better study your Bible. There are hundreds of good Bible studies available. It is hard work. To live on spoon-feeding from the preacher is one of the dangerous results of wanting to feel good. Generally it feels pretty good to sit and listen effortlessly.

Our daughter keeps asking, "Have you mentioned the 'think machine'?" Sometimes at our house we remind each other to "Put it through the 'think machine.' " Often a little reasoning goes a long way. It was easy to get past my irritation in the traffic jam by simply reasoning that only tension could result from my continued irritation (and all the big things tension brings, headaches and so forth). I decided to sing—it's always safe in a car! Major decisions take more time to think through.

The helping person is invaluable at this point. The heavy feelings of sorrow or temptation or fear are out in the open where they can be looked at; their power is somewhat dispelled and the thinking process can be activated. Be careful with whom you share. If it's someone to whom you really feel the need to say, "Please don't tell anyone," it's probably because you know that person is a poor risk. (Sometimes, though, I say that to a true confidant only to reassure myself that my "secret" is safe.) If you're sharing a temptation, it's probably better not to share it with someone involved in your temptation unless it's a person of great integrity. If you're tempted to tamper with the funds, the president of the company is probably not the best person to tell. If you're tempted by your neighbor's wife or husband, probably neither of them is your best choice for sharing. Of course I'm assuming in all the matter of sharing that you really want to be rid of the thing.

Growth can be stopped if decision isn't carried out. The courage, the determination that may be necessary is the price of new growth. The decision to do something, particularly if it involves meeting someone eyeball to eyeball (a confession, for instance), can immediately give rise to more uncomfortable feelings, even acute ones. If you've arrived at your decision scripturally, thoughtfully, with integrity, I know nothing helpful short of plowing ahead with what you've decided to do. Having decided, does it ever feel better to try to forget it? Probably not. God promises even the right words in hard places.

Deciding seems to me the most complicated and far-reaching step in the process. It puts feet on the first two steps (when decision is necessary), and produces both inward and outward fruit. It's also the step that brings us into the battle between sin and righteousness.

The word *honest* keeps coming to my mind. "Honesty" is sometimes paraded in a foolish way, as when you feel righteously honest about telling Mrs. Brown her wig is atrocious, or brag that all of your life is an open book to everybody. Real honesty recognizes all that we are. It puts names on "bad" feelings as well as "good" ones. It accepts (however sadly or grudgingly at first) that they belong to us. It acts in light of God's standards. It keeps on making necessary efforts. "And for that [seed] in the good soil, they are those who, hearing the word, hold it fast in an honest and good heart, and bring forth fruit with patience [perseverance]" (Luke 8:15).

Some Positive Feeling Words

I feel...
I am feeling...

appreciated, admired, encouraged, approved, liked
understood, valued, important, worthwhile
all right, comfortable, content, relaxed
ambitious, assertive, bold, determined, zealous
surprised, astonished, awed
expectant, hopeful, optimistic
friendly, neighborly, warm-hearted, companionable
brave, courageous, daring
carefree
calm, tranquil, serene, peaceful
cheerful, glad, enthusiastic, exuberant, merry, overjoyed
gentle, kind, tender, concerned, considerate,
    compassionate, pity
cooperative, dependable
curious, watchful
sensual, desire, lust, ecstasy
excited, thrilled
generous, hospitable
inspired, creative
interested, understanding, sensitive, sympathetic
gracious, merciful
tenacious, determined
transparent, open
independent
unbiased
sentimental, romantic
serious, sensible, reasonable
confident, self-assured, sure
pleasure, enjoyment, satisfaction
alive, eager, vibrant, energetic
safe, secure, belonging
longing, yearning
grateful, thankful

Some Negative Feeling Words

I feel...
I am feeling...

timid, afraid, fearful, terrified
cross, grouchy, indignant, exasperated, mad, furious, angry
edgy, apprehensive, uncertain, alarmed, worried, anxious
aloof, indifferent
uncaring, callous, unconcerned
baffled, muddled, perplexed, upset, confused, bewildered
hesitant, cautious, reluctant
suspicious, threatened, hurt, defensive, attacked
stubborn, obstinate
listless, half-hearted, lethargic
discontented, gloomy, grim, despondent, morose
tired, wilted, pooped, exhausted
bored, dull, blah
greedy, miserly, grasping
embarrassed, shy, self-conscious, inhibited
envious, jealous
dislike, disdain, aversion, contempt, abhorrence, hate
impatient, aggravated, annoyed
mean, merciless
shaky, uneasy, panicky, desperate, helpless
neglected, friendless, lonely, unwanted, desolate, forlorn
misunderstood, misjudged, martyrish, bitter
mangy, mousy, shabby
insecure, out-of-place, different
fussy, meticulous, officious
pensive, moody, melancholy, resigned
mediocre, inferior, incapable, inadequate, incompetent,
    worthless
undone, unglued, overcome, hopeless
inflexible, intolerant
tense, uptight, paralyzed
foolish, ridiculous

suppressed, oppressed, trapped
stretched, pressed, worn thin
touchy, picky, squeamish, thorny

Notes

1. J. R. R. Tolkien, *The Fellowship of the Ring* (New York: Ballantine Books. Edition arranged by Houghton-Mifflin Co.).

Feelings and Becoming Whole

11

I used the word *whole* very glibly in some early writing. Reading it, a friend circled the word and said, "What's that?" I felt irritation because he knew better than I did about "wholeness," and I hadn't thought it through.

In Matthew 5:48 Jesus said we must be perfect, as our heavenly Father is perfect. Translations differ—one uses "good" rather than perfect. Perhaps "whole" is another such term. Each of these words challenges exhaustive definition. In its context in the Sermon on the Mount, Jesus was turning his listeners away from a simplistic definition of perfection, telling them they couldn't be complete even if they followed the old law very closely, that perfection as they saw it was beyond them, a challenge far greater than they suspected.

Having become aware of feelings, knowing they are part of all we are, there is no way that we can with integrity consider wholeness without taking the existence and importance of feelings for granted. A great gain in wholeness comes when we learn to recognize, accept, and handle our feelings. Then they assume their rightful role: to do their work quietly and well. Of course we feel them, but with wholeness we no longer need consciously to consider them at every turn—as is necessary when we're becoming acquainted with them. When we have learned to drive a car, much of it is done automatically, but we still need to be conscious of what is happening. When we are well on the road to wholeness, our thinking won't be muddled by confused feelings, just as our judgment in driving isn't sidetracked by confusion between brake and clutch.

Becoming whole will always involve our feelings because it involves change, and we can't change without feeling it. We feel insecure when we're testing new ground. We may feel rejection when our growing interferes with our relationships. We will feel pleasure when growth comes. It feels good to look back and see growth, even if the stretching itself has some negative feelings attached to it. Never underestimate the role of feelings in all the ways of becoming whole; feelings are evident in the parts of wholeness we will now consider.

We can approach wholeness by imagining that it is like a sphere, cut in half. Wholeness is half how I relate to myself and half how I relate to another person. We can enlarge this idea in thinking about relationships with others: one half is how I relate to myself and to you, the other half is how you relate to yourself and to me. So each of us as persons can reach a large measure of individual wholeness (relating inside to ourselves and outside to others), but in another sense, wholeness is dependent on other whole people relating back to us. Elizabeth O'Connor turns this principle around: "To the extent that we are lost to ourselves, to that extent we are lost to the world."[1] There is a large measure of satisfaction in the process of becoming whole as a person. The satisfaction is enhanced when, as a growing person, I am in vital touch with someone else who is also changing, becoming complete.

Becoming whole certainly begins within, with knowing oneself and experiencing God. Wholeness grows with awareness of a living, developing relationship between oneself and God. It has its existential roots in a God who says, "I was ready to be sought by those who did not ask for me; I was ready to be found by those who did not seek me" (Isaiah 65:1).

In both spiritual birth and growth, there is no ultimate answer to becoming whole apart from meeting God. As Paul Tournier puts it, "The spiritual life consists only in a series of new births."[2] We keep confronting God in Jesus Christ in every new step. In one of the Narnia chronicles of C. S. Lewis, a thirsty girl has seen a sparkling stream, but a great Lion lies between her and the water. Twice she is invited by the Lion to come and drink. She continues to hold back.

> "Are you not thirsty?" said the Lion.
> "I'm dying of thirst," said Jill.
> "Then drink," said the Lion.
> "May I—could I—would you mind going away while I do?" said Jill.
> The Lion answered this only by a look and a very low growl.... The delicious rippling noise of the stream was driving her nearly frantic.
> "Will you promise not to—do anything to me if I do come?" said Jill.
> "I make no promise," said the Lion.
> Jill was so thirsty now that, without noticing it, she had come a step nearer.
> "*Do* you eat girls?" she said.
> "I have swallowed up girls and boys, women and men, kings and emperors, cities and realms," said the Lion...
> "I daren't come and drink," said Jill.
> "Then you will die of thirst," said the Lion.
> "Oh, dear," said Jill, coming another step nearer, "I suppose I must go and look for another stream, then."
> "There is no other stream," said the Lion.[3]

Both the intimacy and ultimacy of our meeting with God make other considerations of wholeness seem incidental.

Yet we know the reality of this meeting only by the fruit that is borne from it. "You will know them by their fruits," said Jesus (Matthew 7:16). A "whole" life does have identifying marks of fruitfulness. To express them on paper is like seeing a barren tree in winter; to see them in a life is like seeing a tree resplendent in summer.

Of course, the life of Jesus was completely whole, so a sound approach to discovering wholeness is to view him through the eyes, ears, hearts, and minds of the Gospel writers. The work of the Holy Spirit in us is to make us like him. But as we cooperate in this process, becoming thirsty for completion, there is some value in trying to identify characteristics and qualities of wholeness to work toward. The following few aspects of wholeness are suggested at random, with no attempt at a progression from good to better.

One mark of wholeness is willingness to give worth to others generously and spontaneously, being able to feel personal worth without the need to ascribe it to oneself. In Luke 7 the Roman centurion is described by the Jewish community as being worthy of Jesus' attention. A little later he is saying to Jesus, by way of servants, "Lord, do not trouble yourself, for I am not worthy to have you come under my roof." We can't attribute this remark to a false cultural humility; a Roman is speaking to a Jew. In Philippians 1:1 Paul called himself a servant while ascribing worth to the leaders of the Christians there, giving them the status of "bishops and deacons." Later he reminded them that he had not "arrived." But on other occasions, Paul's healthy sense of personal worth allowed him to tell people that they could use him as their example. A feeling of worth is only as good as the character it reflects, but it is nonetheless an indispensable ray in the spectrum of wholeness.

Another part of becoming whole is the ability to move next to a hurting person, to feel another's pain and not be afraid of our own reaction to it. I remember countless instances of my husband being called to help in situations of great turmoil when I was devoutly thankful that he was the minister and not I. It wasn't that I was too sensitive to bear pain; the truth was that I managed most often to erase it altogether. I simply didn't know how to relate to it. I recall the first time I met the crisis pain of another without fear. It wasn't because I'd experienced that pain myself. But after I began learning to handle negative feelings, identifying my hurts and angers, it released me to approach others. My fear of another's pain is gone, but I am still not able to call myself whole; there is pain in the world that I'm not sure I could cope with.

Wholeness is maintaining one's individuality while keeping a balanced eye on the scriptural truth that we are one body in Christ. Being "individually members of one another" means looking not only at our own interests, but also at the interests of others. Yet it means allowing each member the freedom and dignity of handling his or her own affairs. When I am most sensitive to my friends' feelings, I will be most quick to obey the "Golden Rule"—to be to them what I would like them to be to me, and from their point of view. We Christians need to learn to allow others to "hear" what is going on inside them, and to express it if they want to, while we are judgment-free. Nor do we help by trying to dispel their negative feelings with positive ones. It doesn't work to cancel negatives with positives—we aren't talking arithmetic. One student described his satisfaction with a particular friend by saying, "He doesn't jump in to try to fix things up when I share problems." It's so tempting to jump in when we know the answers good and well!

One part of wholeness begins when I recognize clearly what I very much want. It moves toward completion in both spiritual and physical realms as what I want begins to be what I have. Paul said, "I have learned, in whatever state I am, to be content" (Philippians 4:11), and "Godliness actually is a means of great gain, when accompanied by contentment" (1 Timothy 6:6 NASB). One step in this process is to get in touch with what we most deeply want, the psalmist's "desires of the heart." It's safe for us to do this. It's healthy to think, "What do I want?" The thing uppermost in our minds at that instant will demand to be the answer. Then think, "Is that what I really want? Do I want all that it would bring with it?" Possibly not. "What is it, then, next layer down, that I want more?" and so on. To get in touch with what we really want is the key to being a productive person. We cannot really die to self, or give our self away, if we haven't begun to hear and handle the demands of self. To find out what we really want is helpful in setting goals and priorities as responsible people. Goal setting has to come from within. We need to be doing what we sincerely want to do; those are the only things we will do genuinely well. Heading toward goals set for us by someone else gives rise to inward battles, scoldings, and defeats. Paul found his "wants" much more trustworthy than behavior based on what he was told to do by the law (Romans 7).

Becoming whole is to move realistically through the immaturities in our spiritual experience to their mature counterparts. If we can't say, "For me to live is Christ and to die is gain," with inner honesty, it isn't a sin. It's just that we're still growing, still becoming complete. It's the principle of Philippians 3:13-15. We work through from the immature to the mature. Psalm 1:2, 3 is another example of wholeness toward which we grow: delighting in the law of the Lord, meditating on it day and night. Paul said, "Pray without ceasing" (1 Thessalonians 5:17). One layer of our consciousness can be occupied with constant prayer; we can be aware of that layer even while involved with other things. I think that the part of our mind with which we could be praying is lost to us when feelings aren't under control. Perhaps unceasing prayer can become a deep desire, an inner goal. We aren't set in cement. We can view the maturities of Scripture, and move toward them if we choose. They can become a matter of anticipation rather than of judgment or discouragement.

Becoming whole is learning to live in love with those who differ from us in Christian doctrine and practice. Bruce Larson said, "Our maturity is seen in our ability to accept a threatening truth that someone else may bring to us about the amazing Gospel of Jesus Christ."[4] It's refreshing to breathe a little of that maturity. Some of today's heavy doctrinal emphases are recent developments. Whatever did the church do without them before? Take, for instance, our specialized views of how history will end and the correct order of events surrounding the second coming of Jesus. Some of us insist on a minuscule principle of the inspiration of Scripture that didn't even occur to anyone until the twentieth century. Let's get the mature feel of a big God and grow toward wholeness by discovering new points of view.

Becoming whole is finding the word *spiritual* stretching honestly to include all of life, learning to recognize the role of God in everything we are and do. We understand that there are earthly things and heavenly things, but Christians frankly given to God don't categorize life in those terms. Food, clothing, sleep, sex, work, and other physical aspects of living are not unspiritual compared with Bible study, prayer, and church attendance. All can be undertaken with ungodliness or all can become avenues to a deeper walk with God. "And whatever you do, in word or deed, do everything in the name of the Lord Jesus" (Colossians 3:17). Of course the earthly and the heavenly are in tension; the Bible recognizes the reality of the upward call and the earthbound fact. "We have this treasure in earthen vessels, to show that the transcendent power belongs to God and not to us" (2 Corinthians 4:7). "Work out your own salvation with fear and trembling; for God is at work in you" (Philippians 2:12, 13). "The life I now live in the flesh I live by faith in the Son of God" (Galatians 2:20). Since the tension exists by the nature of things, it's wise not to create more tension by trying to add a phony spiritual dimension. We frequently do this, for instance, by using the Lord's name to impress people. We may use it out of habit, in a thoughtless way. (But it's no mark of genuine Christianity to exclude his name from all conversation in reaction to those who over-spiritualize.)

One mark of wholeness will be how we meet the rapid and radical changes that are taking place in our culture. To say that wholeness will "meet change without fear" ignores the reality that fearful times will come and we will feel them. There is much that is dreadful about the decline in our culture, but Christians have a special role to play. A missionary reporting on the behavior of Indian Christians during the months of fighting between Hindus and Moslems, before the separation of India and Pakistan, said that because the hope of the Christians was in another world, because their ultimate salvation was not staked in their country's political and religious struggle, they could go about as healers—helping, bringing comfort, keeping steady. Christians will always be privileged to be healers, to be calm and purposeful in times of turmoil.

As you think about wholeness, other dimensions of it will come to mind. Maturity is a lifelong work, undertaken best in the context of faithfully living out each day, with what God gives us to do. As we go about our activities, God meets us and provides his measure of blessing and growth. Abraham's servant, acting in obedience, was successful in finding Rebecca for Isaac. The widow of Zarephath was gathering sticks to cook her last meal when Elijah came. Amos was among the shepherds of Tekoa when he was called to prophesy. Zachariah performed his duty in the temple and God revealed his will. Paul was serving God to the best of his zealous being when he was stopped in his tracks on the way to Damascus. Lydia and her friends were worshiping in the light they had, and then God brought them new revelation. In this context of daily life I would like to consider one more aspect of becoming whole.

Notes

1. Elizabeth O'Connor, *Journey Inward, Journey Outward*, p. 59.

2. Paul Tournier, *The Adventure of Living* (New York: Harper and Row, 1965), p. 39.

3. C. S. Lewis, *The Silver Chair* (New York: Macmillan, 1953), Chapter II.

4. Bruce Larson, *Living on the Growing Edge* (Grand Rapids, Michigan: Zondervan Publishing House, 1968), p. 15.

Wholeness and the Adventures of Life

12

The last mark of wholeness considered here may be the most important. It has to do with the twenty-four hours of our day. We experience big and little adventures every day. How we handle them is basic to all the other ways wholeness develops.

As time marches on, "dramas" come and go. It's a mark of wholeness to let all of our dramas move on so that new ones can come. Paul Tournier talks about "the law of adventure, which is that it must die," and "the death to which every adventure is inevitably subject."[1] He is including all of life's adventures, the joyous as well as the painful.

Early in this book, feelings were described as good simple tools that anyone can use to grow in faith. We know that when tools are worn out and can no longer be used, they need to be laid aside. This is true with feelings in the happenings of our lives. Some feelings are automatically set aside by the flow of events. For instance, there is the "cloud 9" joy of the birth of a wanted baby. This feeling floats while relatives and friends are aroused to the blessed event, it fills the room through all the first fondling of that little bundle, it shines like the sun through the smiles of Mother and Dad. It's replaced only hours later by the solid feelings accompanying responsibility and the return to routine. The real yet euphoric first feelings seem to evaporate like a fleecy cloud.

Many special events in life are like this, encased in a particular time span: reunions, parties, vacations, illnesses, minor failures, setbacks. Unless these have taken on dramatic proportions, the feelings that go with them may be important and linger a little, but they pass.

At other times, a crisis situation invades our lives. A major matter of life is involved. A great Fact can develop within, or be forced on us from without, or both. By no means do we always have control of the shaping of our own great Facts. The Fact could be the death of a beloved person. The Fact could be that your children, who have claimed your choicest attention and time, are now leaving home. The Fact could be a divorce. The Fact could be that you have forsaken "house and family and land" for foreign soil, and the initial gratification and excitement are gone. The Fact could be an involvement in business or in relationships or in any other area of life that must be put away. The possible Facts are innumerable. Consciousness of such a Fact can lie in a wakeful state just beneath the surface of all life's superficial but needful demands. For most people, overwhelming feelings will surround their great Fact. Emotional involvement becomes intense. And it must be remembered that what is crucial and inundating to me may be simply melodramatic to you—so far removed from your experience that you might label it foolish if I tried to make you understand. Woe to the one who has the privilege of hearing, and then labels quickly what he hears. That is the person who doesn't really "know," who isn't in touch with feelings, to whom judgment is more familiar than compassion.

Regardless of the direction from which our great Fact has come, no matter who is responsible for its existence, there is a sense in which we hold our crisis in our own hand. Behind the Fact, the feelings are ours to handle. We work and rework the feelings that threaten to overcome us. They are intimate companions night and day. We talk to God. Hopefully we talk to friends. Time goes by. The Fact-crisis crests quietly within, or events outside us allow it to culminate. Gradually the conviction dawns that we're keeping in our hands a "feeling tool" that is wearing out. The edge has been taken off the knife, the tool has served its purpose. The feelings of grief, emptiness, loneliness, alienation, bitterness, or temptation have lost their power.

In life's desirable adventures, we face the wearing out of the feelings in the same way. The elation, enthusiasm, thrill, concern or optimism of our positive happenings wear thin. In either case we become sure that an old adventure must go. The decision to open our hands and let it go is ours to make.

Someone might say, "No, I can't. I can't open my hand and let it go. There is simply not that quality of strength in me." Are you willing? God, who has all the skill for drastic surgery, won't decline to perform for you. It is at this point of willingness, I think, that we must each decide who is the liar—myself or God? Jesus said, "I am the door; if any one enters by me, he will be saved, and will go in and out and find pasture" (John 10:9). It's possible that the thing, the Fact, keeping us most forcibly is also the thing that we most want to be rid of. The experience is a crescendo of giant breakers against the rock cliff, the confusion of the coming together of willing and wanting and feeling. But there are "deciding places," moments of truth. It isn't a mystical thing. This opening of the hand, this desperately thin place for deciding, can be in secret or in the company of loving or skilled people. But it must happen.

We have come again to the freeing quality that a decision gives us. The decision comes when we're ready to move on with life. It has the feeling of health because it's something we can act on. We can stop doing a thing or do something different. George MacDonald, writing "A Letter to American Boys,'' talks about decision. He is writing in a room while facing a small empty stage which he says will soon be filled with actors. Then he says, "It looked to me like a human heart, waiting to be filled with the scenes of its own story—with this difference, that the heart itself will determine of what sort these groups shall be."[2] Groups of people, plans, ideas, hopes. The heart, filled with emotions, has a great deal to say about decision, and when decision comes, the corner is turned, the direction changed. It's possible that the turning will be a matter of repentance. The strategic battle is won. The occasional skirmish or backward glance is unfulfilling, the memory dims, the will is toward a new call, a new commitment. The feelings fade.

The Christian's success in meeting the major dramas is a great boost to faith. We experience the kind love of God which bears with us and suffers with us through what seem endless and faithless days. Or we sense his pleasure in our enjoyments, and our faith in him grows beautifully. But decision is only as valid and practical as the steps that go before it. The "sure success" in finally letting go of a major adventure we have lived with intimately can come only when two things have happened. The first is that we have worked through the feelings surrounding the crisis. This is crucial because they are the voices that hang on after the crisis itself is over. It's important to let feelings "have their say" inside. We engage in a new battle if we pledge to ourselves, "Now I'll never feel that again." We are such perverse creatures that a declaration like that is a challenge to ourselves. It awakens the whole feeling area.

The law that we learn to handle all feelings alike applies here; failure to recognize and work through the negative feelings that go with the awful crises means failure to enjoy to the hilt the positive happenings. To the parents of that newborn infant who are in touch with themselves, there is consciousness of the happiness. The new feelings that come as they move on aren't a letdown, but feelings of a different kind. The special feelings surrounding the baby's birth don't actually disappear, but are allowed to become sweet memories. We are free to enjoy life's great glad moments while they last. We are free as well to let them go. When the orchids have turned brown in the refrigerator, there can be a positiveness about placing them in the wastebasket.

Along with working through the feelings, another thing must happen before we can let go that large Fact we have lived with. We must unconditionally accept whatever is going on inside. The principle of acceptance of the "unacceptable" in our lives is a difficult one to grab hold of and hang on to. It seems like asking us to approve of something we simply can't. "Acceptance" and "approval" sound alike, but they're not. I must accept what is reality in my life; I can't let go of what I've never completely held on to, just as a child can't wholeheartedly give away something until he has established his ownership beyond a doubt. I must identify with my reality. I am not above or better than my most "unacceptable" things. They are where I am; they are, in fact, me.

I experienced this about a month after beginning this chapter. I had been working through something "unacceptable" and I announced to a friend my success in overcoming it. He said, "Perhaps you've accepted it." I immediately felt bristly and impatient inside, because I felt he was saying that I did approve of it, after all. He wasn't saying that, but the feeling I had confirms to me how ingrained is the idea that the negatives in us are bad. Later that day, and all of the next, the thing I had "gotten rid of" was bothering me again. That was frustrating because I was writing about "letting go" of our outworn happenings and I wanted my insights to be workable. Then I remembered that when I'd first admitted and accepted what was going on in my life, it was "conquered." Now when I felt superior and above it, back it came. Renewed acceptance almost immediately brought peace.

A friend who generally is cheerful seemed distressed one day and I asked her about it. She was feeling a lot of resentment and bitterness as a result of something someone had said to her months before. Periods of peace would come because she had asked forgiveness, but just when she thought the problem gone, back it would come in a flood. She wholeheartedly wants to be right with God. But she will have no lasting peace until she accepts those negative things, until she's willing to stoop to the idea that they really belong to her, that there's a sense in which it's "all right" to feel as she does, that those are morally neutral emotions. She has done nothing sinful except beat herself. Nothing fruitful can come of it unless it drives her to the foot of the cross. Our most "acceptable" things are no better at the cross than our "unacceptable" things, our "unacceptable" things no worse.

A large part of humility is the willingness to see ourselves honestly bereft of goodness. It is accepting all the feelings we dislike in ourselves, but doing it without defeat and hanging our heads. The cross is not there for defeat. It is the place we meet God's grace in our naked condition, and he clothes us. I am moved by the comments of Bishop Kivengere on Jesus' meeting the woman at the well. She went to that well because at the common wells in the town she couldn't stand the other women, "the eyes that stripped her naked." When she encountered Jesus, "for the first time the eyes of this broken woman met the eyes of God in human form.... His eyes did not strip her, they actually covered her up, invited her near."[3]

One of the most authentic marks of wholeness is acceptance of our not having arrived. But, "The farther you go, the nearer home you are."[4]

To *read* that feelings are "all right," that it's good for Christians to be human and to enjoy being ourselves, is an academic exercise. To *know* that negative feelings aren't sin, but are instruments to be used by us in our partnership with God in the process of becoming, is still theoretical. To read and to know can begin to relieve and release. But only learning and practicing, unlearning and practicing some more, in a spirit of self-acceptance, will cover the territory up ahead. It may take months; the progress may seem imperceptible.

We have so much to get rid of, so many old habits to overcome. We have an enemy in the camp, because Satan wants to keep us from renewal. But God wants us to move along the dark corridor when there is no light. He wants us to open our eyes so we can see the thin ray that will inevitably come and dispel the gloom. He wants us to rejoice in the warm sun. Do you see yourself in one of those stages of the journey? Do you see yourself in more than one place at the same time? It is all part of the adventure, and God wants us to get on with it.

Notes

1. Paul Tournier, *The Adventure of Living*, p. 21.

2. George MacDonald, *The Gifts of the Christ Child* (Grand Rapids, Michigan: William B. Eerdmans Publishing Co., 1973), Vol. I, p. 11.

3. African Enterprise *Outlook*, Vol. XII, #5, May, 1975.

4. MacDonald, *op. cit.*, Vol. I, p. 184.